SAM WELLER'S BOOKS
BOUNTIFUL
NO CASH REFUND

28 MAR '84

·4 *	·5.00	*
·4 *	·5.00	*
·7 *	·18.95	*
·4 *	·2.00	*
·4 *	·1.50	*
·4 *	·1.00	*
·4 *	·1.00	*
TxA	·34.45	*
TX	·1.98	*
B · *	·36.43	ST
62 B · *	·36.43	CT

28 MAR '84

```
A  . . . . . .  5.00  *
A  . . . . . .  5.00  *
T  . . . . . .  18.95 *
A  . . . . . .  2.00  *
A  . . . . . .  1.50  *
A  . . . . . .  1.00  *
A  . . . . . .  1.00  *
TA . . . . . .  34.45 *
TX . . . . . .  1.98  *
B  . . . . . .  36.43 ST
B  . . . . . .  36.43 CT  2#
```

From the Crossroads...

Other Books by Richard L. Evans

♦

UNTO THE HILLS

THIS DAY . . . AND ALWAYS

. . . AND "THE SPOKEN WORD"

AT THIS SAME HOUR

TONIC FOR OUR TIMES

FROM
THE
CROSSROADS...

by
RICHARD L. EVANS

HARPER & BROTHERS, PUBLISHERS
New York

TO ALICE AND OUR FOUR SONS
who have helped to make life
sweetly cherished, always—and forever

"May peace be with you,
this day—and always."

Contents

[7]

[8]

SOME PLAIN TALK ON TEACHING

TO YOUTH LOOKING FOR A FUTURE

SOME QUESTIONS OF CONSCIENCE AND COMPENSATION

OF PEACE AND REPENTANCE

ON SURVIVING SORROWS

[10]

Foreword

"**B**efore the H-bomb, before the atomic age, before World War II, before 'the long Presidency,' before Hitler, before the Japanese seized Manchuria, before the Great Depression and even before the Wall Street crash, long, long ago, July 15, 1929, a great 375-voice choir began broadcasting coast-to-coast from the Salt Lake City Tabernacle."

—thus *Life* Magazine began its editorial noting the twenty-fifth anniversary of "Music and the Spoken Word from the Crossroads of the West"—which this same quoted source says "is the oldest coast-to-coast sustaining program in existence."

Hardly can we believe it has happened, but already we are writing and speaking on our second quarter century of this traditional Sunday morning CBS broadcast "with the Tabernacle Choir and Organ from Temple Square in Salt Lake City."

And so we offer this volume of two-to-three-minute "chapters" (the sixth such volume to be published), with grateful acknowledgment to all our listeners, to all our associates, to all who have helped, to KSL, to CBS, to the Tabernacle Choir, and to all others also.

To continue quoting from the *Life* anniversary editorial:

"Those who know this program (Sundays, CBS, 11–11:30, EST) need no arguments for listening to it, or no introduction to its producer and commentator, Richard L. Evans, or to the choir's director, J. Spencer Cornwall, or to Organists Schreiner and Asper, or to the disciplined voices of the farmers, grandmothers, businessmen, high school girls and other devoted Mormons who make its enormous sound. Millions have heard them, and more millions, we hope, will hear them in years to come. It is a national institution to be proud of, but what matters more is that Americans can be linked from ocean to ocean and year to year by the same brief respite from the world's week, and by a great chord of common thoughts on God and love and the everlasting things." *

The contents of this book concern themselves with that "great chord of common thoughts on God and love and the everlasting things." And we are grateful for the things which thoughtful men have in common which come from the Father of us all, who made us in His image.

May peace be with you—each and all of you—this day—and always.

R.L.E.

* Excerpted by permission from *Life* Magazine © Time, Inc., 1954.

On Seeing Things Through

"A door must be either open or shut." [1]
—French Proverb

On Seeing Things Through

One of the indispensable elements of a sincerely successful life is the ability, the power, the capacity and the willingness to see things through—to carry things beyond conversation to conclusion. And one of the disappointing qualities of character is the failure to see things through.

There is usually no scarcity of suggestions as to what should be done; there is seldom a scarcity of conversation; but there is often a scarcity of coming to conclusion.

One of the colorful characters of history may be cited as an example of one who seemingly finished very little in life. Leonardo da Vinci ventured into innumerable scientific and artistic areas. He theorized, experimented, speculated and advocated ideas far beyond his day. But the tragedy of his life is said by some to be the things he could have done but left undone—the things he failed to follow through.

The Lord God has given us life—and time and energy and materials and intelligence—and an assured reward for carrying things to conclusion: for keeping the commandments and not merely discoursing upon them; for doing the work of life, and not merely theorizing—for producing something solid. And the half-done tasks, the work begun and set aside, the incomplete projects, the frequent dropping of tools to loaf and let time waste away, the futile appearance of houses started and left partly completed, are all evidence of the premium that is and should be paid for seeing things through.

One day we shall all return to Him who sent us here, to give an account of our accomplishment; and concerning some things we might have to say; "This we almost did." "This we might have done." "This we didn't do."

But how glorious and satisfying to be able to say, "This we have done." "These are our works." "These are the crops we have planted and harvested." "These are the buildings we have built." "These are our children." "These are the men we have helped." "These are the lives we have lifted." "These are the commandments we have kept."

It is easy to see why there are rich rewards for enduring to the end, for finishing the course, for completing life's projects, for following through.

Excuses

O ne of the obvious evidences of man's inge-
nuity is the excuses he contrives to make.
The variety and plausibility of our explanations to
ourselves and others for our failures to perform
sometimes seem to exceed the fabrications of fiction.

We explain why we didn't continue a certain
course, why we didn't finish school, why we didn't
pay a debt, why we don't break a bad habit, why we
dropped the ball, why we were late, why we weren't
there, why we didn't accept an assignment, why we
failed in marriage, why we didn't keep our word,
why we didn't keep a commandment, why we
departed from a principle, why we didn't deliver
on the promised date. We can explain them all—
these, and ten thousand other things—sometimes
sincerely, sometimes superficially.

Admittedly excuses are often valid and sincere
and acceptable. Courts of law recognize that there
can be valid reasons for failure to perform. There
are acts of God, so-called, and of men, and circumstances and situations which make it physically,
practically, literally impossible to do some things we
should have done or said we would do. There
are laws that give relief to the person who has done
his best and who finds it impossible to go beyond his

best, and we should have no undue fear of facing our ultimate just Judge if we have lived up to the best of our understanding and opportunities in the circumstances in which we found ourselves.

But not so with him who confronts his friends or fellow men or his eternal Father with specious, shoddy, superficial excuses for his failures. And this we must remember: No matter how good an excuse may be, no reason for failure or defection is ever so satisfying to ourselves or to anyone else as is actually doing what we should do, or delivering on the date that something is due. Excuses are at best a second-choice substitute.

It is a surpassing quality in life to follow through, to keep commitments, to keep the commandments, and no matter how ingenious our excuses are, they don't cancel commitments, or justify our failures, or relieve us from answering before the highest bar, unless they are founded on real, valid reasons—and not merely on our comfort or convenience.

On the Fringe

In thumbing through some commonplace words we find *"fringe"*—and we find it thus in part defined as "an ornamental border . . ." or "something resembling a fringe; . . . as the outer fringe of a crowd."

No doubt there are fringes in almost everything; but as to actual performance, fringe doesn't seem to play a very important part. It is there. It may look well—but it is only on the edge. And that in part describes people who are "on the fringe," as well as the fringe on fabrics.

Families have their fringe. Clubs and committees have their fringe. Communities and countries have their fringe. Churches have their fringe. Every organization, every institution has its fringe of those who hang out on the edge. They aren't altogether in or altogether out. They claim to be part of the picture when there is something good going on but refuse to be part of the picture when there are obligations to be borne.

They want the advantages of citizenship without assuming their full share of service. They want the privileges of membership without meeting their due measure of obligations. They want the love and loyalty of the family without carrying their full share of the family load. They want the blessings and benefits of the church without conformance or service or support. They want the freedom, peace and protection and prosperity of the country without giving full loyalty or allegiance.

Surely there is some stigma in just staying on the edge and never quite being part of the picture. And one wonders how much patience the Judge and Father of us all will have with those who choose to live their lives on the fringe, without becoming a real functional part of the fabric.

The larger blessings and promises of life (as well, indeed, as lesser ones) are predicated upon performance, upon participation, upon the doing of the thing, upon the living of the law, and when we do what we should do, we shall somehow, somewhere, receive the promised reward. But if willingly we fail to perform, if willingly we are found on the fringe, if we cannot quite be counted in or out, we shall fall far short of full effectiveness—and far short of the compensations that come to those who can be counted on.

On Being Where We Ought to Be

When we are supposed to be doing something we don't do, often we have to argue with ourselves inside. A man has to give himself a reasonable reason for what he does or fails to do, and if the reason isn't a good reason, it may involve an uncomfortable contest between two sides of himself.

This is true in all our obligations and activities. When we don't live up to the best we know, when we don't deliver the best we can, when we aren't present where we are supposed to be present, when we aren't doing what we ought to be doing, we have to keep telling ourselves why; and this kind of conversation takes off the edge of every enjoyment—like a brooding, threatening cloud that hovers over a picnic; like intrusive noise in the background when we are trying to listen to music; like an interrupting voice when we are trying to engage in quiet conversation. An uneasy conscience is a discordant obligato that detracts from all sweet sounds.

A man simply cannot keep his mind on his work with full effectiveness when he has to keep telling himself why he doesn't do what he knows he ought to do, why he doesn't go where he knows he ought to go, why he doesn't keep appointments he knows he ought to keep, why he disappoints people he knows he ought not disappoint, why he lets small causes and small excuses dissuade him from more important pursuits.

Actually it often takes more time to talk ourselves into and out of the things we ought to do than it does to do them. And often we actually save time and greatly increase our effectiveness and efficiency if we simply decide to do what we know we ought to do and then set about to do it.

To all of us—and to young people particularly—let it be said again: Being where we ought to be when we ought to be there, doing what we ought to do when we ought to do it is one of the indispensable factors of success, of effectiveness and efficiency, and of personal peace. It avoids the necessity of inside argument and often takes less time than the time we take telling ourselves why it is all right not to do what we know we ought to do.

The Agony of Indecision

There are two things in life of exceeding importance: one is to decide, and the other is to decide right. To be torn between two alternatives without being able to make up one's mind is a time-consuming, peace-destroying factor that can do much to nullify effectiveness.

As we look back upon the plight of Hamlet with all his troubles and sorrows, one of the things for which he was much to be pitied was his agony of indecision—his hanging between "to be or not to be."

But Hamlet isn't the only one who hasn't been able to make up his mind. Even in the lesser things of life, even when circumstances aren't so serious, most of us wrestle with ourselves in the gnawing agony of indecision: whether to go or whether to stay; whether to buy this or to buy that; whether to accept this proposal or another one; whether to take this job or some other; whether to go back to school and finish what we have started, or to postpone our preparation; whether to take the trip or give it all up.

Sometimes decisions are made by default; that is to say, sometimes we simply sit and wait and worry until time has taken the choice out of our hands.

That's one way of deciding—by simply not deciding. But if we do this too often, we live too much of our lives in the agony of indecision.

All of us have to make many choices—every day, every hour, sometimes it seems almost every instant —some serious and some superficial. And if all of the right factors are on one side and all of the wrong factors are on the other, deciding should be a very simple matter. In matters of principle, of morals, or ethics, or honesty there is really only one choice—or should be.

But in other matters, sometimes it isn't so simple. Sometimes there are things to be said on both sides. Sometimes we have to weigh one against the other and give up something either way—and these are the difficult decisions.

But we need to decide—because hanging between two alternatives does much to waste time and to nullify effectiveness. And when we seem to hang in uncertainty, there are some things that may help to settle us: one is a set of sound principles. We all urgently need a sound set of principles by which to measure everything. We need to know the rules, the law, the commandments. Another thing we often also need is someone we can trust to talk to. And beyond our own wisdom and the wisdom of others, we need faith—faith and a prayerful approach to all our problems.

God grant that we may have the wisdom and the faith to save ourselves from wasting life away in the agony of indecision.

Concerning Simple Solutions...

Many centuries ago, Isaiah implied that there would be certain ways marked out for men—marked out so plainly that "wayfaring men, though fools, shall not err therein." [2] There are many purposes and principles so plainly marked out that men *need* not err therein, but it sometimes seems that the simple answers aren't what is wanted.

Rube Goldberg, creator of cartoons, has given us many an illustration of the needlessly complex means men sometimes seek to arrive at simple solutions; for example, a man may devise a complex mechanism that will tip his bed up—and him out of it—at a certain time in the morning. But a much simpler solution would be simply to set the alarm clock, and then have the courage to get up when it goes off.

It will be remembered from mathematics that a straight line is the shortest distance between two points. But it sometimes seems that we want to wander around in the wilderness: that we want prescriptions with unpronounceable names; that we want to explain things in wordy ways—to speak in legalistic language, when a simple statement of right or wrong would often be much better; that we want to go far around in explaining economic processes and procedures instead of seeing (or accepting) the simple fact of cause and effect.

As suggested by William Faulkner, some of the solutions to some of our problems are much more simple than is sometimes supposed—not necessarily easy (not even perhaps, particularly palatable) but simple—as simple as spending less than we earn, as simple as leaving a bad habit behind, as simple as truth and honor and honesty and integrity, as simple as repenting—as simple as the Ten Commandments, as simple as the Sermon on the Mount, as simple as the Gospel of the Man of Galilee.

The fact is that simple honesty, simple humanity, simple economics, simple laws, simple commandments, will, if kept, offer the solution to many of our most pressing problems. That's what is frequently meant by getting back to first principles.

There may be no absolutely painless way of solving a grievous problem. There may be no really painless way of repenting—or of paying debts. There may be no easy, effortless way of working for what we want. There may be no altogether pleasant and palatable way out of anything—but there may be a simple way, if we will face the facts and not try to do everything as if it didn't really have to be done.

* * *

"He that shall endure to the end, the same shall be saved." [3]

—Jesus of Nazareth

A Sound Sense of Values

"All good things are cheap; all bad are
very dear." [4]

—Henry D. Thoreau

"Mark the End..."

There are times and moments in life when people seem to have arrived at what they want—when the plans and purposes they have pursued seem to have been successful. But this we learn, sooner or later: that life is not a single scene. It is a series of scenes. It is not a portrait or a static picture—it is a moving picture, and not a matter of any single moment. And just when we think all the pieces are in place, something may happen to change the pattern and the picture.

To turn for a moment to history: Napoleon, in the period of his ascendancy, is said to have written a boasting letter concerning the solidness of his situation. But Lord Nelson, into whose hands the letter fell, added a three-word postscript to it: "Mark the end." [5] Mark the end—and the end of that episode came later with the defeat of Napoleon's fleet.

"We know what we are," wrote Shakespeare, "but know not what we may be." [6] One successful scene doesn't necessarily make a successful plot or a successful play. A play is composed of many parts and is not over until the final curtain—all of which suggests humility as a becoming quality: humility among men, humility before God, for we none of us know when success will sour, when happiness will

[31]

turn to sorrow, when health will turn to sickness, when affluence will be altered by accident or adversity.

So changeable is life, so varied are the shifting scenes, that no matter who we are, or what we are, or where we have arrived, we none of us know when we shall have need of other men—or need for help beyond the help of men. And a smug sense of superiority, inconsideration of others, taking unfair advantage, abusing power, abusing position, all these and many other things unmentioned have often proved to be but the prologue to a different kind of scene and sequence.

The tides of all things turn, and before we can surely say someone is successful, we should know how far and how consistently he can carry success. And before we smugly assume that we are unassailable, we would well remember Nelson's postscript to the boasting words of Bonaparte: "Mark the end." ". . . he that shall endure to the end, the same shall be saved." [7] God help us to remember that life is not a matter of one scene, but an endless and eternal sequence of scenes.

On Relying on Laws
and Locks

On the question of being safe with someone:
After all other considerations are taken into
account and given their proper appraisal, we had
just as well, first and always, face this fact: that the
only things we can count on ultimately are honesty,
integrity, and high qualities of character.

There is no such thing as being permanently
safe simply with laws or with locks. No lock was
ever made that gives full and lasting protection
against a cunning and determined dishonesty—because the same kind of brains that can make a
so-called safe lock can outsmart a so-called safe lock.
The same kind of brains that can make a code can
break a code. The same kind of mind that can
devise a so-called "fool-proof" system, can, if determined to do so, outsmart a "fool-proof" system.

Laws and locks retard dishonest people, but they
don't stop dishonesty. Only honesty can stop dishonesty—only integrity, only high qualities of
character. And whenever we have to put ourselves
in someone else's hands, as we often do, whenever
we have to trust people in any occupation, in any
profession, in any relationship in life, we should

look beyond skill, beyond talent, beyond personality, beyond appearance, beyond ability—beyond all these (but including them also if we can) we should look for qualities of character. And if we can't count on character, there is very little that we can count on.

No man has reason to sleep very well if his whole trust is placed in locks and alarms, for people have proved repeatedly, with boldness and craftiness and cunning, that they can invade the most safely guarded precincts; that they can perpetrate multi-million dollar frauds upon the public; that they can circumvent accounting systems, audits and rules and regulations. And with more laws and locks than we have ever had before, and with more men checking on other men, there is more and ever more violation of laws and of locks.

Too often, in too many places, too many of us have too much put our trust in mere physical factors, in the arm of flesh, and have too much forgotten the inner make-up of the man. But when we have found someone with high qualities of character, someone without evil intent, someone who knows the difference between what is his and what isn't, what is honorable and what isn't, we have found a possession beyond price—for one of the greatest blessings of life is someone to trust, someone to be safe with.

Balance and Specialization...

The Tower of Pisa has been famous for centuries because it has stood so long while leaning some sixteen feet off center. In this it is an exception—for most towers that have leaned that far have fallen and are no more remembered. Balance in life is one of the essentials of safety, of happiness, and of wholeness. Lack of balance has been the cause of more misery and mistakes than men can calculate.

In academic activities, in professional pursuits, and in other occupations also, young people—most people—are mostly dealing with material matters. By the very physical necessities of life, by the fact that we must be fed and clothed and sheltered, many, if not most of us, are largely devoted to a consideration of physical factors. Our reading, our thinking, our living are largely along these lines.

This is a day of specialization, and to "succeed" it seems that a man must know more about some things than he knows about others. He must be able to do some things better than he is able to do others. But specialization can be carried to a dangerous degree, and can lead to an educated illiteracy—an illiteracy which knows of some things to the latest letter of the law, and of other things too little—an

[35]

illiteracy that could find itself on far tangents along narrow little lines.

There are so many tangents that could take us far from the truth as well as those that could take us toward it, and for a wholeness of life we all need to temper our thinking, and to keep a balance in every avenue of every activity—with time and place for prayer, for acquaintance with the timeless truths of scripture, and thoughtfulness for the great eternal intangibles as well as for the things that we can touch. Every person is a composite being, with an immortal spirit within, and for a fullness of life we must feed the spirit as surely as we must feed the flesh.

Tangibles we cannot take with us, but intelligence and love and spiritual qualities we can. And no matter what a person's particular pursuit, he should be ever aware of the need for a wholeness of life, for a wholeness of understanding—for balance.

Balance—and Bias

On this question again of balance: Almost anyone, if he will let himself, can bring himself
to seeing only one side of a subject—the side he
wants to see. Debators, for example, may at first
approach a question without prejudice, but as they
concentrate on the side they are assigned to, their
vision can become almost as if someone had placed
blinders upon them, and they see only the evidence
that favors their side and fail to see (or fail to give
due weight to) the evidence that favors the other
side. And soon they have built, what is to them at
least, a convincing case. And others who are assigned to defend the opposite side can become
equally convinced in an opposite direction.

This is only one illustration of how men may
become overbalanced if they confine themselves to
restricted facts or disregard evidence which seems
to them to be pointing away from where they want
it to point.

This brings us again to the hazards of extreme
specialization, and again to the question of what
could be called "educated illiteracy." Will Rogers
once remarked that "there is nothing so stupid as an
educated man, if you get him off the thing he was
educated in," [8] which was merely his homely way

of suggesting that because a person is an expert in one field he is not necessarily an expert in others also. It is not safe to assume that because someone knows one thing well he knows all things well.

And this brings us again to a point of advice to young people: that in their studies, in their pursuit of understanding, in all their activities, they do not put blinders upon their eyes and look only down narrow lines, and assume that the tangent they are on encompasses the whole sphere of eternal truth.

There are so many unanswered questions. There is so much that none of us knows, that all of us together do not know. And one of the great and invaluable lessons of life is to learn to live a well-balanced life, and to learn to know that when we have seen a small segment of something, we haven't seen everything there is; and that when we have followed one little line of evidence, we haven't yet found a fullness of understanding. There is danger in presuming to arrive at final conclusions with insufficient facts.

"Little Brass Nails..."

Perhaps all of us pursue some things which, after we acquire them, seem somewhat shallow or shoddy or at least unessential. And then we wonder why we wished for them so much and worked for them so hard, and passed up more worth-while things we might have had.

There is a parable by John Ruskin that has much to suggest concerning this subject. He said it was a dream, but we rather surmise it was a dream he deliberately dreamed for the purpose of putting over a point:

"I dreamed," he said, "that I was at a child's . . . party, in which every means of entertainment had been provided . . . by a wise and kind host. . . . The children had been set free in the rooms and gardens, with no care whatever but how to pass their afternoon rejoicingly. . . . There was music . . . all manner of amusing books . . . a workshop . . . a table loaded with everything nice to eat . . . and whatever a child could fancy . . . but in the midst of all this it struck two or three of the more 'practical' children that they would like some of the brass-headed nails that studded the chairs, and so they set to work to pull them out.

In a little while all the children, nearly, were

spraining their fingers in pulling out brass-headed nails. With all that they could pull out they were not satisfied; and then everybody wanted some of somebody else's. And at last the really 'practical' and 'sensible' ones declared that nothing was of any real consequence that afternoon except to get plenty of brass-headed nails. . . . And at last they began to fight for nail heads, . . . *even though they knew they would not be allowed to carry so much as one brass knob away with them*. But no! it was, 'Who has most nails? . . . I must have as many as you before I leave the house or I cannot possibly go home in peace.'

At last they made so much noise that I awoke, and thought to myself, 'What a false dream that is of *children*. . . . Children never do such foolish things. Only men do.'" [9] And so ended Ruskin's dream of the children and the little brass nails.

One of the greatest gifts of God is a sound sense of values. It is a gift of inestimable worth for those who have a limited time to live—which, so far as the limits of this life are concerned, includes all of us. And yet, even as the foolish children referred to, it would seem that much too much of our time may be taken in struggling for little brass nails, which we cannot take home with us at the end of the day.

At Another Person's Pace...

Perhaps most of us have had the experience of trying too closely to follow another car; and soon we learn how hazardous and difficult it is, how tense and trying, to drive at another person's pace. To be safe and effective, and to enjoy the driving, we have to feel the road for ourselves.

In other things also, people are often made unhappy and uncomfortable by trying too hard to proceed at another person's pace. Critical comparisons can make men most unhappy—and the whole course of life could become frustrating and ineffective by assuming that one person should precisely duplicate the performance of another person.

Sometimes parents make insistent comparisons between their children, and assume that one should closely follow the pattern and personality of another. But despite strong family resemblances, children are usually more different than identical. We all came here different. Every man is an individual—eternally so. Without laboring the fact, let it simply be said that we are in part the product of our pre-existent past—and our talents and intelligence didn't begin within the limits of this life. Furthermore, with our God-given freedom, one person may not choose to move in another person's pattern.

Sometimes trying too closely to follow our neighbors' pattern causes unhappiness and hazard—especially financial hazard. This counsel came to one young man: "Do not run faster or labor more than you have strength and means: . . ." [10] Competition and energetic effort are very much worth while. They improve people, and they improve standards of performance. But trying to live our lives in the precise pattern of other people can be wasteful and unwise.

In the Saviour's parable of the talents, the penalty imposed on the man who had one talent was not for his failure to have five but for his failure to use what he had.[11] The Lord God does not expect us to be identical with anyone else. He knows us and expects us to be ourselves. (If we aren't ourselves, we aren't much of anything at all.) Nor does He expect of us perfection. But having given us freedom to feel the road for ourselves, He does expect us to be our better selves. He expects of us an honest, intelligent performance, with repentance and improvement—and not too much repeating of our own past errors.

If Washington Were Here...

On the surface it might seem that we today have few of the problems of Valley Forge, and that they had few, if any, of ours. But the principles and the problems that pertain to people basically are quite constant. And if Washington were here, we can only conclude that he would not retreat from any principle which he turned to in facing the troubles of his own time.

If Washington were here, no doubt he would still say (as he did in his own day): "Reason and experience both forbid us to expect that national morality can prevail in exclusion of religious principle." [12]

No doubt he would still say: ". . . cherish public credit . . . avoiding likewise the accumulation of debt, not only by shunning occasions of expense, but by vigorous exertion in time of peace to discharge the debts which unavoidable wars have occasioned." [12]

If Washington were here, no doubt, he would still say: The "Constitution . . . till changed by an explicit and authentic act of the whole people, is sacredly obligatory upon all." . . . "It is important . . . that . . . those entrusted with . . . administration . . . confine themselves within their re-

spective constitutional spheres . . . [for] usurpa-
tion . . . is the customary weapon by which free
governments are destroyed." [12]

If Washington were here, he would still speak
out against irreverence and profanity and would
still seek divine help in prayerful humility and
would still commit his own life and his country's
future to faith in free men.

Admittedly the land he led through some of its
early anguish was not then and is not now a place
of perfection. Admittedly the land he led still has
its problems. (As have all other lands.) But its problems, significantly, are partly the problems of
plenty, and with its problems, blessedly there is also
unsurpassed opportunity. And should we ever become unconstructively critical, or overly discouraged by some of the problems and some of the setbacks, it would be well to ask ourselves if anyone
honestly would want to turn back to the philosophies our fathers fled from, or if anyone honestly
would want to turn toward those other philosophies
which millions of men today would risk their very
lives to leave?

If Washington were here, we believe he would
say: Avoid the paths that lead to that which other
men fervently wish they were free from. Avoid the
principle of compulsion. Keep faith in freedom.

Thank God for Freedom

May we take a moment from some of the side issues and from some of the irrelevant celebration, and clear our thoughts and humble our hearts and get down on our knees and simply, fervently, thank God for freedom—and then get on our feet with a firm resolve to preserve it against all who secretly or openly would set it aside.

Thank God for freedom—and for the Founding Fathers who reaffirmed to a new nation, an eternal, timeless truth: that the right of choice—that the free agency of man—is a God-given inalienable right, and is essential to the peace and growth and progress and salvation of the very soul.

This truth has been challenged again and again, and will yet be challenged again and again. It was challenged in the heavens before time began, by the brilliant but rebellious Lucifer. There was war in heaven—for freedom. And anyone who seeks to enslave men in any sense, in mind, in spirit, in thought—anyone who seeks to enslave the minds, the hearts, the spirits of men is essentially in league with Satan himself—for "where the spirit of the Lord is, there is liberty." [13]

Thank God for the Constitution of our country, which was brought into being "by the hands of wise men whom [the Lord God] raised up unto this very purpose." [14] Thank God for the promise that in this choice land, men "shall be free from bondage, and from captivity, and from all other nations under heaven, if they will but serve" God.[15]

Thank God for the right of choice, for the right to become whatever we can become in a free and provident land that, despite its imperfections, has proved to be more efficient for progress and human happiness than any society founded on the false philosophies that would seek to enslave the minds and souls of men.

God grant that we may repent wherever we have departed from the principles of freedom—that we may preserve the right to fail and the incentive to succeed, and live, as did the Founding Fathers, knowing that there are no acceptable substitutes for freedom.

If We Were to Die on a Definite Date...

In making decisions or in meeting emergencies, it is sometimes significant to see what a man is most concerned to save. In case of fire, for example, it is interesting to observe what each man considers to be his most priceless possessions.

In one way or another, all of us are daily demonstrating our sense of values by what we do or fail to do, by what we buy or refrain from buying, and by every use or misuse of time and talents and opportunities. When we lose our health, we feel that we would give anything to have it back. But when we have health, we often shamefully abuse it in careless or unwise conduct. Many men lose limbs and even life while taking needless chances in seeking to save lesser things. Sometimes they lose life in the attempted saving of a few seconds.

But if we were given a month to live and knew that this was all we had left of this life, it would be significant to see what our choices would be. And it would be safe to say that some of the things we have been pursuing, and some of the things to which we have given top priority on our timetable, would be quickly shaken down in their order of importance. And some of the things we have neglected would quickly move up toward the top.

Some of the visits we might have had with our children, some of the talks with loved ones we might have taken time for, some of the obligations we might have met, some of the commandments we might have kept, some of the worth-while things we might have worked at—all might be hurriedly revaluated if we knew that time were to be taken from us on a definite date.

"I know of nobody," wrote Thomas Fuller, "that has a mind to die this year." [16] Yet always there are before us inevitable eventualities that come for some sooner, and for some not so soon—but ultimately for each of us. "It is a poor thing," said Tertullian some seventeen centuries ago, "for anyone to fear that which is inevitable." [17] Nor need we fear, if we keep before us a sound sense of values, and recognize the sham and superficialities for what they are, and keep our houses in order and cherish our loved ones, and work at worth-while things, and walk humbly with Him who is the Father of us all, and do our best to evaluate all things as we likely would if we knew that the time allotted us here would end on a definite date.

Suddenly It's Autumn

I don't know how it is where you live, but where we live there has been a different feel in the air these past few days. By sure and certain signs we are well aware that suddenly it's autumn—as trees begin to shed their summer dresses, leaf by leaf, first having costumed themselves in high color to celebrate the autumn evening. And one of these mornings the grass will be white and crisp. Then the fields will take on quieter color, before winter steps in and covers the sleeping silence with white sheets.

Aside from the beauty, the naturalness, the wonder of this annual occurrence, what always strikes us is that it comes so suddenly.

We remember only yesterday hearing the children talk of being soon out of school—but the summer has suddenly slipped by, and now they are back again at their books.

We remember only yesterday watching the last snow melting, and farmers plowing spring fields. Only yesterday, we remember looking anxiously for the first sign of leaves to show.

Only yesterday (or so it seems) we remember the rush of Christmas shopping, and the ever-fresh wonder of the Christmas morning; the new year; February and valentines; April and Easter; May and

Memorial Day; June and commencement; and July and August; then summer is gone—and suddenly it's autumn.

Wonderful as it all is, yet too many summers have slipped suddenly from us without our having done a thousand things we had intended to do—things we had solemnly said "this year" we would do, with family and friends—when school was out, when summer came. But summer came and slipped away—and suddenly it's autumn.

And too much of life itself has slipped away, as spring has successively succumbed to summer, and as successive summers have suddenly passed. And when it is autumn, it is almost winter; and when it is winter we had better have the harvest behind us.

Scrambling for lost time is an unhappy occupation. We can buy the harvest of the farmer's field. We can buy apples by the bushel. We can buy all the material things that another man has made. But in life we cannot buy a year or a month or a minute. And with the seasons and the years slipping from us so suddenly, surely we should sharpen our sense of values; surely we should look at everyone and everything around us and ask ourselves what really matters most.

* * *

"For what is a man profited, if he shall gain the whole world, and lose his own soul? or what shall a man give in exchange for his soul?" [18]

—Jesus of Nazareth

On Becoming Bored
with Work

"I never did anything worth doing by accident, nor did any of my inventions come by accident; they came by work." [19]
—Thomas A. Edison

The Law of Harvest—the Law of Return

Here is a simple statement of the law of harvest, of the law of return: "Cast thy bread upon the waters: for thou shalt find it after many days." [20] In plain, inelegant language, it is the law of putting something into something before we expect to get something out of something.

Basically, unselfish giving, working, serving, is in a sense an enlightened sort of selfishness, for it carries with it the certainty of receiving. But the man who tightly withholds himself, who seeks altogether to "save" himself, his effort, his energy, to get without giving, to hold tightly to everything he has, will undoubtedly, as any miser must, be found among the most impoverished of people as to the things that matter most.

It is trite to say so, but still inescapably true, that "whatsoever a man soweth, that shall he also reap." [21] And we should not expect to have a harvest without working and waiting; we should not expect to receive dividends without saving and investing—nor to acquire skill without practice, nor knowledge without study, nor reward without work.

[53]

We must not expect friends without offering friendship, nor kindness without giving kindness, nor understanding without offering understanding —and we must be ready to give first, and not expect others always to make the first move. In other words, we must be willing to put in before we expect to get out. And the attitude of holding back, of never making the first move, of "saving" ourselves, in a niggardly sense, constitutes a kind of stifling stalemate.

Someone has to have faith, and the willingness to wait—faith enough to put in the fuel before the wheels begin to go, faith enough to save and invest before the dividends come due, faith enough, and foresight, and wisdom, and understanding and kindness and hospitality, and bigness of heart to make the first move in friendship, in love, in service, and even in common courtesy.

Someone has to have faith in men, faith in the future, faith enough to learn, to work, to save, to invest, to wait—faith enough to give of himself before he begins to get. And as surely as the law of return, the law of compensation operates, and assuredly it does: "Cast thy bread upon the waters: for thou shalt find it after many days"—with an increase of it also.

On Becoming Bored
with Work

"I thank God each morning, that I can get on the bus and go to work." Thus a recent thoughtful visitor, explained his blessings with this simple sentence.

Simple as it is, or at least simple as it sometimes seems, to have constructive work to do and health enough and strength enough to do it, is one of the greatest blessings of life. And should we ever doubt it, we need only see someone who hasn't work or who hasn't his health.

Sometimes we might wish we had work we liked better. But sometimes the solution to this is to learn to like better the work we have, to learn to enjoy what we are doing or must do.

Frequently, we hear young people express themselves as being weary of some assignment, perhaps some course at school, or practicing on the piano, or learning the "times tables," or learning to type, or some other routine task. They complain that such things become boring. But almost anything can become boring—even some things that seem fascinating at first. Almost any boy, for example, would like to run a power mower—for a few minutes, but not to keep at it hour after hour, day after day.

Even so-called thrills can become boring. Life itself can become boring—if we let it. But we can't always go from thrill to thrill. We can't always go from excitement to more and more excitement, to the more and more spectacular, to the more and more extravagant. We can't limitlessly add more and more spice to give an ever added edge to the flavor of food. There is a limit to the amount of spice that can be put in without completely forfeiting the natural flavor. Besides, the human constitution can't constantly and increasingly take it.

And so it is with living, and so it is with work: It is wonderfully rewarding to learn to enjoy the work we have, at least until we find what we like better. It is wonderfully rewarding to learn to like what we must or should do (as well as what we think we would like to do)—to learn to enjoy the simple, the solid, the sustaining things—home and life and loved ones, and the wholesome things around us, and not become bored with our blessings.

Serendipity

There is a word in our language, an unusual word coined by Walpole, but little known and little used. It is *serendipity*—which means essentially: something unexpected that you find along the way when you are looking for something else.

Many of the world's discoveries and much of the world's progress have been brought about through avenues that have been opened when someone was seeking to discover something else—by facts that have been found when someone was looking for other facts.

Columbus is one of the great historic examples. Countless such accounts could be given, not confined to the discovery of continents and geographic areas, but in all of the sciences, in all of the professions, in farming, mechanics and manufacturing methods—and in finding friends, in personal things, and even in spiritual experiences.

There are innumerable things that men have discovered, that men have developed, including talents and resources and abilities, because they have kept working and moving, and searching and seeking when they could scarcely see the first step—and certainly couldn't see the ultimate end.

There are by-products in every process. One thing

leads to another. One step suggests the second. And the fact that we can't see through the last door need not prevent our opening the first door in any constructive search.

To few men has it been given to see very far into the future, but to make the most of life a man must keep moving and working and searching and seeking for better ways and finer things, for knowledge, for light, for truth, for understanding. ". . . seek, and ye shall find; knock, and it shall be opened unto you." [22]

If we are not in search of something, we are less likely to find anything. If we are not working at something, we are less likely to make anything. If we don't keep moving, we are less likely to arrive anywhere.

We have to make the decisions of each day to the best of our ability and face the future with faith. And if we keep trying, if we keep moving, we often find rewarding things that we little expect—things which we never would have found in idleness or inactivity or indecision.

The Question of Retirement...

To be able to close each day with a sense of accomplishment is one of the greatest blessings and precious privileges of life, one that entitles a person to sound sleep and sincere satisfaction as few other things do.

But sometimes men work, having foremost in mind the wish to be free from work. Then through some circumstance the time may come when they are, in a sense, free from work—and then they find that the idea has much less allure than they had once supposed.

Of course there is such a thing as overwork and too much pressure. And under pressure there is some tendency to swing to the other side and to place a fictitious value on retirement. But the word itself, *retirement*, sets up a false set of standards if it means inactivity and idleness. There may properly be retirement from some pursuits, a change of activity, a lessening of responsibility, a change of pace or position. But work has been accused of too many ills.

When a man needs a rest, very often it isn't that he so much needs a rest from work as a rest from worry, a rest from pressure. Men rust out sooner than they wear away; they wither in idleness sooner than they break down in willing useful work.

Friction will wear us away—friction with other people, friction within ourselves. Pressure and impatience will do their damage. A bad conscience will wear a man away. Worry will wear a man away. But willing, constructive work, within the limits of one's health and physical strength and talents and time, is a lengthener of life and a catalyst without which there is little real happiness.

Freedom from work in the sense of doing nothing constructive or of having nothing constructive to do, is a false standard; and unfortunate is the person who has forced time on his hands—time that he must fill with forced pleasures and hollow pursuits.

The right to work is a blessing that should gratefully be accepted and earnestly safeguarded. And work, itself, with a sense of accomplishment and of usefulness in life, is the surest safeguard against wasting away.

The Pursuit of
Pleasant Pastimes

Often we complain about being busy, and certainly at times we are—too busy—sometimes at essential things and sometimes at nonessential things. And because we are so busy, we may sometimes wish for inactivity, even for idleness; we may wish for the leisure to pursue what have come to be called pleasant pastimes. But before we sever ourselves from definite assignments, before we turn away from work, before we disengage ourselves from real responsibility, we should take a realistic look at what are sometimes called pleasant pastimes.

There are times for all of us when leisure is essential, for rest and refreshment. And there may be times when even the avid pursuit of pleasure seems attractive on the surface. But actually people sometimes pursue amusement and synthetic pleasure to the point where it is more work than work is. And sometimes it seems that a considerable part of the people are working at relieving the boredom of another considerable part of the people who are bored because they aren't working.

Why this great effort anyway to pass time? As the poet said, so each of us could say: "O time too swift! O swiftness never ceasing!" [23]—a swiftness ever swifter, at whatever age we are. And some of the so-called pastimes and synthetic pursuits only press us faster along a road which already we scarcely seem to sample before we leave the years breathlessly behind. From now till next week will seem in its shortness almost as if it were tomorrow morning. And it seems ironical that men should so persistently pursue the so-called pastimes when time, which is the essence of all our opportunities, is already running a race which it always wins, without any synthetic assistance.

And as to pressure, as to being busy: it is so much better than not being busy that we may well be grateful for the urgency that presses us into constructive pursuits.

Work... and Worry...

There are situations and circumstances that would prematurely wear us all away if we would let them. There are rough, eroding experiences that, with some of us, leave raw, deep wounds, but with others seem somehow to heal sooner or not to cut so cruelly.

In some we sometimes see so tight a tenseness that the wearing process is painfully apparent. And then, in contrast, we sometimes see someone who has lived through not less—but who has somehow learned to live with comparative freedom from the full effects of some of life's frictions.

We all have hurts; some of us harbor them. We all have misunderstandings; some of us magnify them. We all have to deal at times with difficult, irritable, unreasonable, unpleasant people; some of us resent them too much and overlook too little. We all have annoyances, frustrations, disappointments. We are all subject to some sorrow, to sickness, sometimes to the loss of loved ones, to unkind comment, to the cutting edge of criticism. No one's life is lived completely free from the conditions that could cause wearing friction.

We all have to make adjustments. But by faith and forbearance, by the patient withholding of judgment, and by being so absorbed in useful work that it leaves little time to brood, we can often avoid the abrasive quality of bitterness, of harsh eroding resentments—and free ourselves of much of the effects of friction, and live longer than we would otherwise live, and be healthier and happier while we are living.

Again it should be said that worry, a bad conscience, pressure and impatience, resentment and unreconciled sorrow all provide the friction that sometimes makes the going rough and raw. But faith, forbearance and work are part of the formula that frees us from friction—faith in the purposefulness of life, in the mercy and love and justice of an Eternal Father, faith in ultimate understanding and complete compensation. Faith, forbearance, and useful, willing work can free us from much of the worry and friction that would otherwise wear us away.

Do the Best You Can...

It is an unhappy day in the life of anyone when he fails to find sincere satisfaction in doing useful things for the joy of doing them—and in doing them to the best of his ability. We all have ambitions; most of us want money; we may want prestige and position—all of which, as Ruskin observed, are acceptable as secondary objectives, but all of which are subordinate in giving satisfaction and in producing essential qualities of character. Superseding them all is the sincere satisfaction of work well done.

Most of us are obliged to work whether we want to or not. But there is an extra premium for taking pride in work—the pride of doing more than simply getting by, the pride of equaling or improving our past performance.

It was the Saviour who said, "Be ye therefore perfect, even as your Father which is in heaven is perfect." [24] It may not appear that this kind of perfection is within the reach of mortal men. But the reaching for it is within reach. And we should not be satisfied with substandard performance. We should not be satisfied with "seconds," but only with a product on which we could be proud to place our label.

[65]

The makers and manufacturers of many things sell "seconds" and substandard products under other names. But a man in his own life cannot hide behind another name. His label is indelibly on everything he does. Even if it isn't actually imprinted on his product, it is imprinted on his own soul, on his personality, on his inner appraisal of his own performance. As one man bluntly fashioned a phrase, negative perhaps but meaningful: "Do the best you can—that's bad enough." [25] We all fall so far short of perfection that less than our best is less than acceptable.

In doing our best, in being at our best, we become better. In doing less than our best, we move backward. And any time we attempt to get by with as little effort as we can, we somehow slip back.

Since we should and must work (and since life moves with such swiftness) it is important that we ask ourselves always whether we are putting out our top product, our top performance. If we can answer affirmatively, we shall have the happiness and surpassing satisfaction that come only with useful work well and willingly done.

* * *

"Fear God, and work hard." [26]
—David Livingstone

The Duty of Being Happy

"Make us happy and you make us good." [27]

—Robert Browning

The Duty of Being Happy

"There is no duty," wrote Robert Louis Stevenson, "we so much underrate as the duty of being happy."[28] We think of happiness as being deeply desirable but seldom perhaps think of it as a duty. But duty it is, for without it life falls short of its full power and purpose.

To attempt to define it would be difficult to do, for its formula varies. And among its paradoxes is this: the happiest people are not always those that one would expect to be the happiest. But there are some essential elements that must go into its making, and lacking any of these, the so-called happiness we have is of a lesser kind and quality.

First is faith, with work, and love, and a quiet conscience. These four together add up to a sense of peace and purpose, and a sense of rightness within—faith in a loving Father who made His children in His own image and who holds before them limitless eternal purpose and progress; faith in the ultimate triumph of truth; faith that wrongs will be righted and that there will come an end to discouraging days—and nights—even if the darkness sometimes makes the dawn seem long delayed.

And then work: There are many kinds of work,

but there isn't much that could be called happiness without purposeful, willing work.

And as to love: This is one of the chief attributes of God, and one of the greatest attributes of His children. Without love there is little meaning in life: the love of friends and family—those special few who have close and special meaning—and the love of others also, all of whom are children of our Father. Love is one of the greatest ingredients.

And then, of course, a quiet conscience, free from a sense of uncleanness, free from a sense of dealing or judging unjustly, and with a willingness to admit errors and to make amends.

It is difficult to define happiness; but we know when we find it; and we know when we lose it; and we know that all men are looking for it. Others may help to make it. Others often impair it. But it isn't something that someone can guarantee to anyone else. It is something that grows inside ourselves, with faith, with work, with love, and a quiet conscience, with peace and purpose and a sense of rightness within. Happiness is indeed a duty, for "men *are* that they might have joy." [29]

Suppose We Lost Everything...

It has sometimes been suggested that to make us fully thankful, everything we have should be taken from us, and then one at a time, each cherished and essential thing should be given back to us again. It would be a shocking, sobering experience at first, but no doubt as our blessings were again bestowed, we would feel an immeasurable greatness of gratitude. But since actually most of us are not called upon to go through any such "shock treatment," suppose that mentally we do so for a moment.

Suppose that in our minds we strip ourselves of everything we have: loved ones, home, health, work, food, friends, freedom. Suppose that in our minds we see ourselves in stark comfortless want—and then imagine, if we can, how blessedly happy we would be if the blessings we now have were returned to us one at a time.

And yet, with all we have, there is often evident among us an inexplicable unhappiness, an inexplicable discontent. It is one of the perplexing wonders of the world that we should sometimes find so much to make us discontented—that we should so much let dissatisfaction keep us from the full and free and thankful enjoyment of all that is ours.

Too often we let unfavorable comparisons make us unhappy and think too much upon what we don't have rather than what we do.

Life isn't utterly untroubled for any of us. There may be loved ones far from us. There may be ambitions we have failed to fulfill. There may be some who seem to get what they have with less effort than others. We are all subject to losing those we love. There are times of sickness and sorrow and setbacks. But despite all difficulties and periods of personal disappointment, thankfully let us face this fact: If we have enough to eat, enough to wear, enough to keep us well and warm, useful work and loved ones, health and home, friends and freedom—and faith—or even if we have most or many of these things that so much matter, we have cause to join with the Psalmist in saying: "My cup runneth over."

If we think otherwise, again suppose we give up everything we have; again suppose we start with nothing and think how grateful we would be for each blessing bestowed.

Happiness—and Success

Happiness is the most pursued thing in all the world. All men are looking for it, whether they know it or not. Our Founding Fathers knew its place and importance when they listed it along with life and liberty. Happiness is properly life's chief pursuit, and there is no special virtue in unhappiness, there is no special virtue in long-faced living.

But like most things, happiness is often misunderstood, often mistaken, and often missed. One doesn't find it always where he might suppose, and frequently finds it where it seems less likely—but whatever its variations from person to person, real happiness always has within it some indispensable essentials, quite apart from passing or trivial pleasures, quite apart from hilarity or lightheaded laughter, or dangerous thrills, or cynical satisfactions.

Sometimes happiness is confused with what is sometimes called success. But success itself may need another look. Success is not just indiscriminately more and more of everything; it is not just indiscriminately going and getting. It is getting what we want—if we want the right thing. It is arriving where we want—if it's the right place. And one could scarcely be considered successful if he isn't happy, and could scarcely be considered happy if he didn't have a wholeness and wholesomeness of life, integrity, work, service, self-respect, appreciation for other people, love, a sense of belonging, a sense of being wanted and a sense of purpose—permanent, eternal purpose, with faith to survive the sorrows and setbacks and faith to outface fear.

Going, getting, arriving—even these are not so essential as is this: an awareness of being on the way, on the right road. This surely is one of the chief essentials of happiness—with an awareness also that life is purposeful, limitless and everlasting, and that the same sound principles that lead to happiness here lead to happiness hereafter.

Hate—and Happiness

Among the long list of things that make men unhappy, none is more devoutly to be avoided than hate in the human heart. And among all the elements and ingredients of which human happiness is made, none of them, nor all of them together, will produce the desired product without love.

The physical factors of unhappiness: ill health and hurts and hardships, and the passing jealousies, the passing anger, the passing envy, failure, discouragement, uncertainty, resentment against injustice—all these may be difficult at times to bear, and may at times seem all but unbearable. But in all of them together there is not so much of malignancy as there is in the unhappiness that comes with hate. Even some deeply serious sorrows may have in them an element of sweetness. At least there are sorrows that mellow men. But there is no sweetness in hate. In hate there is only a hard and an ever yet harder hardness.

Even punishment in hate misses its purpose. With hate we can hurt or harden a person or crush him completely. But the punishment that more likely leads to repentance and improvement is "by persuasion, by long-suffering . . . and by love unfeigned; . . . reproving betimes with sharpness

[75]

. . . and then showing forth afterwards an increase of love toward him whom thou has reproved, lest he esteem thee to be his enemy." [30]

There may be some who seem to be deserving of hate, but there is no one who can afford to pay the price of hating, because of what hating does to the hater inside himself. It is a poison that compounds other poisons in a literal, physical sense. Besides its mental, emotional and spiritual ravages it does damage to the very physical make-up of a man.

Hate voids the other virtues. With it there is no peace, no happiness. With it there is meanness from man to man.

These are written as being foremost among the commandments: "Thou shalt love the Lord thy God with all thy heart, . . . and thy neighbor as thyself." [31] We may give alms and admonitions; we may keep other commandments; but without love there is sterility in the letter of the law; without love the hearts of men are hollow; but with it all things may be made bearable. But he who lets hate have hold of him will be destroyed by it, if he doesn't control and conquer it.

Some "Psychosomatic" Medicine

We sometimes use formidable words to express simple ideas. Consider, for example, the word *psychosomatic*. While its common use may be relatively recent, its essential idea of the effect of mind over matter, over happiness, over health, is certainly not new. Many centuries ago a man of much wisdom suggested the sense of the subject in a simple scriptural sentence: "A merry heart doeth good like a medicine. . . ." And then he added: "but a broken spirit drieth the bones." [32]

It is easy to prescribe, but it isn't always easy to administer the "medicine of a merry heart," for there is often much to make hearts heavy. There are sorrows; there is sickness; there is sin. There are disappointments, cruelty, unkindness; the loss of loved ones, and loneliness. And if we would, we could easily succumb to the negative side and shut out the sunlight and become darkly depressed. But if we did, we would be overlooking one of life's chief purposes and ultimate aims, for the pursuit of happiness is one of the rights that is inalienable.

This principle hasn't always found understanding or acceptance, but if we will look at the essential facts, we shall see that it is basically so: for we are here on earth as children of a loving Father who has blessed us with the privilege of life and with all else that is ours. And surely the purpose of a loving Father for His children would be sincere happiness.

It is true that we sometimes receive (and no doubt sometimes deserve) discipline. It is true that some of us sometimes mar our happiness by our own foolish, strongheaded acts and utterances. And it is true that some of us might sometimes be subject to unhappiness that we don't seem to need or that we don't deserve. But these things we shall sometime understand (as we now understand some of the purposes of our parents which were not so understandable to us in our younger years).

And if we will keep faith: faith that our Father intends peace and progress and sincere, sound happiness for his children; faith in the purposefulness of life, which is limitless and everlasting; faith in the purpose and power of God to give to each of us complete compensation—with such faith we can survive the hurts and heartaches, with a "heart that doeth good like a medicine."

Prescription for
the Heavyhearted...

Sometimes we suffer the symptoms of diseases we don't have. And sometimes we suffer the symptoms of unhappiness for insufficient reasons. Often unhappiness comes from overemphasizing the negative side of situations. This is easy to do, since time seems to move more swiftly when we are happy and more slowly when we are heavyhearted. And so we might suppose that we are unhappy more than we are.

Life isn't easy at all times for any of us. And if for someone else—if for anyone else—it seems to us to be so, it is only because we don't know enough; it is only because there is a side we fail to see. We are all subject to uncertainties and to some adverse circumstances, some in one way, and some in another.

Furthermore, no matter what we have, it seems that there are always some things we want. But those who have what we want—or what we think we want—are not necessarily happier than we are.

Happiness is not confined to any material set of circumstances. It is not guaranteed by affluence or ease. It is not the monopoly of any place or people.

[79]

Its component parts, or some of them at least, are faith and work, gratitude, a sincere purpose, a sense of being wanted, and the ability to see the hopeful side.

All these elements are indispensable, but faith and useful willing work would seem to underlie all else—faith in the purpose and providence of God, faith in life, and in its everlasting plan and purpose —and work: work not only to satisfy physical wants, but work for the sense of service, and for the sense of accomplishment—work because men are so made that they cannot be as happy without willing work as they can be with it. The right to work is God-given, and the obligation also, and the necessity for it is inherent in man's very nature.

Paradoxically, there is another element that enters in, and that is this: Some of the people we think might not have cause, comparatively, to be as happy as some others, are often among the happiest, most grateful people there are, perhaps because their sense of values has been stripped of some of the superficialities, perhaps because they have learned the great blessing of simple essentials.

It all adds up to the fact that we have more reason to be happy than we sometimes suppose, and to realize it we need only lose some of the things we have—or see someone who has never had some of the things we have—and we may well find the contrast convincing.

On Getting What
We Ask for...

No doubt we have all observed children who insist on having something they see right now—something they have their hearts set upon. And for the moment life seems very unhappy if they can't have, right now, what they want. But patience is one of the lessons of life that must be learned—patience and a sound sense of values; patience and an awareness that there are some things that won't matter so much tomorrow as they seem to matter today.

Perhaps all of us at times set our hearts upon things that later don't seem to matter too much—and forget some things that matter much more. There is evidence, as we move through life, of a shifting sense of values. A child plays with a toy for awhile—a toy he thought he had to have to be happy—and then tires of it and tosses it aside and turns his attention to something else which in turn is also tossed aside. And in this the child is not so different from adults.

Some of the things we insist upon, some of the things we feel we have to have, aren't, in perspective, what they seemed to be, and sometimes some of the most sobering lessons of life are the lessons we learn when we get what we ask for, when we get what we insist we have to have to be happy.

It was Paul who wrote "for we know not what we should pray for." [33] Often we know not what we should want; we know not what we should ask for, what we should give our lives to, and often when we get what we thought we wanted we learn that it wasn't really what we should have wanted, but somehow we couldn't see it sooner.

Life here moves quickly, and with all of its promises, and pleasures, and possibilities, these swiftly moving days are but the brief prelude to limitless and everlasting possibilities that lie beyond. With all our reaching, with all our wanting, with all our using of time, with all our running deep into debt, we would well remember not to overreach ourselves, not to let our hearts become too set on things which, if we had them, would not assure our happiness— and which might make us miss the things that endure, the timeless things, the things that matter most.

* * *

"Happiness is much more equally divided than some of us imagine." [34]
—C. C. Colton

What Makes
a Good Marriage?

"The greatest discovery of my generation is that human beings can alter their lives by altering their attitudes . . ." [35]

—William James

To You Who Begin
Life Together...

Songs of spring and love and of undying devotion
are good to the ears of all of us. There would
be much missing, much emptiness without music
and moonlight and romance. But lovely as all these
are, there must be much more than all these for
the making of a lasting marriage, for the making of
a good and solid life, and for keeping alive the
sweetness of life.

In June we may walk together holding hands,
with adoring eyes and high hearts. But many precious things are perishable if they are not under-
stood, not nourished, not carefully cultivated. Life
isn't all serenity. It changes pace. It changes color.
It is sometimes light and lovely, sometimes difficult
and sobering. There are fair and pleasant days;
there are days of illness, of disappointment, sometimes of sorrow. The covenant of marriage does not
contemplate that any of these will make any difference in loyalty and love. Marriage is not only for
the brighter moments, not only for the prosperous
and pleasant days, but for all the days there are,
endlessly and forever—and it cannot well be built
on less than common ideals, common purposes, full

[85]

willingness to rear a family, usefulness, and sincere service. And no one should marry with the remotest possibility in mind that the ties might sometime be severed.

And you who begin life together: Don't let any unkind comment or act of inconsideration start its widening wedge between you two. There will be moods you will not understand; you will try each other's patience at times; there will be differences. No two people however much in love think or act in all things altogether alike. Don't let differences grow, don't magnify them, don't brood about them; bring them into the open; face facts fairly.

Avoid hasty words and quick condemnation; reserve judgment; build each other and never belittle. Avoid extravagance; live within your means; trust and be true to your trust. Forgive; forget; don't let the errors of the past keep coming back to drive a wider wedge. Be prayerful and patient; live with faith and forbearance; be a blessing to each other always and forever, and don't lose the loveliness of looking down the years of life together. Hold to what you have in June and let it be so, sacredly and blessedly in December.

The Dotted Line...

Signing on "the dotted line" has come to be a symbol of entering into obligations—a symbol sometimes of getting into things that are not easy to get out of. Many have discovered that it is much easier to get into things than it is to get out of them. Sometimes we seem to set our hearts on opening certain doors, on entering into certain situations, and we knock and pry and push and almost insist on getting inside. Then we may find that being inside isn't quite what we thought it was. And often we find that the exits aren't so easily accessible.

This question of getting into what is hard to get out of applies to many matters: to borrowing, to signing notes, to contracts of many kinds, to joining things, to accepting things, to mortgages, to marriages. It is so easy to sign, so easy to accept, so easy to say "yes," so easy to make commitments— and so hard to fulfill, so hard to pay back, so long to regret, so long to repent—so easy to get into and so hard to get out of.

Often we pursue mirages. We follow fashions; we cling to pride; we stubbornly set ourselves, and make commitments and shortsighted decisions. But before we do, we should see ourselves on the paying side as well as on the receiving side. We should read the fine print; we should take a long look, consider consequences, and not commit ourselves to any course that would impair our peace, our solvency, our self-respect, our credit, our character, our conscience.

It isn't only the moment that matters. It is the morning after, the month after, the year after, the long years ahead, the whole of life—and everlasting life.

We must look beyond the moment, through all the days there are, to the day the debt is due. We must look beyond the limits of time, even into eternity, and keep ourselves as free as we can from questionable compromise, questionable company, questionable commitments. We should read the fine print; take a long look at life (and not trust the moonlight too much), and consider all commitments carefully in the clear light of day, and proceed slowly before assenting, before signing.

* * *

"Keep thy eyes wide open before marriage; and half shut afterward." [36]
—Thomas Fuller

On Altering Attitudes

There is a profound thought in these words of William James: "The greatest discovery of my generation is that human beings can alter their lives by altering their attitudes of mind." [37]

This is one of the great discoveries of any generation—or of any individual—and in one sense it is simply a restatement of the principle of repentance. There are times when most of us have need to alter our attitudes. There are times when the stubborn set of a mind or of a heart will drive people apart when they should come closer—and when without some honest change of attitude there would be little possibility of improvement.

Sometimes misunderstandings settle into stalemated situations because neither party will change the set of his jaw, the set of his heart, the set of his thoughts—because neither will alter his attitude. Granted that there may be grievances (and remembering also that no one is perfect), there still must be some honest altering of attitudes, some giving by someone in some degree if resentments are ever to be resolved, if personal relationships between estranged people are ever to be improved.

A person may sincerely feel that it is not his place to make the first move. He may feel that it is not his place to go halfway—or any part of the way. He may sincerely feel that the fault lies wholly somewhere outside himself. But someone has to move. Someone, sometime, has to break the heartbreaking deadlocks of opposing personalities if they are ever again to be compatible. Someone has to do something if what shouldn't be is ever to be as it should be. Someone must make some move if misunderstandings are not forever to remain.

To repeat the words of William James: ". . . human beings can alter their lives by altering their attitudes . . ." Where something should be done, let false pride be pushed aside; let people who should not be apart move toward one another; let repentance enter the picture; let men make the most of life by honestly altering false attitudes.

The Deeper Kind
of Differences

For you who have already made your marriage, there is simply this to be said: Make it work. In marriage there is no ready-made formula for success. It requires character and consideration, honor and understanding, faith and forbearance. No two people were ever alike enough to avoid adjustments altogether. And no two people were ever able to make one another over altogether. Once a marriage is made, make it work. Make a home. Rear a family. Find your happiness in what you have, and in times of trouble look not to see how the ties can be severed, but how they can be saved.

And now as to you who are not yet married, to you who may not be until another June, another year, or another time far future: Because marriage so completely and so permanently affects the lives of all concerned—the lives of the living, the lives of those yet unborn, the lives of children, of loved ones, and of society itself—in this one step one could hardly look too far ahead—at the lasting kind of likenesses—at the deeper kind of differences.

The ideals we have in our hearts, the principles by which we move and make decisions, the convictions we have concerning life, the very grain of our belief, so affects our sense of values, our choices, our very peace and purpose, that, in the constant closeness of living life together, every act and every utterance could either smooth the course of life, or go against the grain. Every standard and every conviction could either combine in common purpose or be opposed in endless argument—an argument of the very soul inside. And with the prospect of a whole life to be lived, of children to be reared, a family to be taught, friends to be chosen, and with endless everlasting considerations even beyond those that we can now foresee, it would be folly to forget disparity of ideals and basic belief.

Again to you who have made your marriage: Make it work. Let petty differences be set aside. But to you whose marriages are unmade: consider soberly the deeper kind of differences and the longer everlasting values.

* * *

". . . marry . . . into a family that will enable your children to feel proud of both sides of the house." [38]

—Robert E. Lee

On Running Away from Responsibility

There are moments when most of us rise above ourselves and our surroundings and sense the glory of service and see beyond the tiresome routine of some of the things we do each day. Those are glorious moments. But perhaps there is no man or woman who lives through life without feeling at times deeply discouraged and weighed down with responsibilities.

Perhaps there never was a mother with her children around her, who couldn't find cause to become discouraged with the work of the home weighing heavily upon her, and with the many unmentioned duties that never quite get done, or that seem so quickly to be undone. And perhaps there never was a father who was faced with the problems of providing for a family who couldn't sometimes feel weighed down with the weight of all that was dependent upon him.

Fortunately we face these things as they come, and usually our power to do grows with what has to be done. But sometimes the load may look too heavy, the tasks too tedious, the work too wearisome; and at tired and discouraging times there may be temptation to run away from responsibility.

Thoreau once wrote: "That we have so little faith

is not sad, but that we have so little faithfulness. For by faithfulness, faith is earned."[39] Blessedly for all of us, our forebears somehow found a way to face their responsibilities—with faith, and faithfulness. And we owe it to the past to do no less in the present, and for the future. No man, no woman, no parent, no provider, no person can possibly find any sincere satisfaction in running away from responsibility. In the first place, anyone who runs away from responsibility loses part of his self-respect. In the second place, he can not run away from himself.

Granted that sometimes some things seem to be all but unbearable. Granted that any household, any assignment, any situation can become trying, burdensome, boring. But life is a test of faith and faithfulness. And for the sake of others as well as of ourselves, for the sake of being able to face our Father in heaven without a sense of shame, we shouldn't run away.

"By faithfulness, faith is earned"—and so is happiness, and so is peace of mind, and so is self-respect. God help us to have the faith and faithfulness to endure to the end—to continue in faithful performance.

Divorce—a Tradition for Failure

There are no two people, however close and compatible, but who could find some occasions of misunderstanding and some causes for annoyance with each other—especially if they become careless and inconsiderate.

In marriage, many things may lead to misunderstanding: differences of personality (peculiarities, we may choose to call them if we are speaking of the attributes of others, and not of our own!), misfortunes, financial setbacks (which all tend to add to the tension), lack of consideration, lack of appreciation (or what seems to be so), and taking too much for granted, letting down, and becoming careless in conduct, and perhaps careless even in personal appearance. And as misunderstandings are magnified, marriages miscarry in mounting numbers, with the wreckage of homes, with hurt and unhappy children, and with little gained by any of it, and with irreparable damage done. The reasons may not always be apparent, but the tragic results almost always are.

Part of the problem may be that breaking up, running away, sometimes seems to be the shortest or easiest solution. But actually it isn't—for without some change inside, the personalities and the problems are simply shifted to another scene, with costs compounded, with endless complications; and the principal participants as well as the innocent bystanders—children and others—are always faced with the fact that there has been a failure. And a tradition for failure is exceedingly hazardous, in families and elsewhere also. A broken home, a broken marriage, always requires explanation. But making a marriage work well is its own glorious beginning of a tradition for success. Marriage is more than a mere social convenience, more than a legal contract. It is a sacred covenant, that cannot, with impunity, be set aside.

Happiness, sincere, mature, stable happiness, seldom if ever comes easily or accidentally. One must work at it, live for it, give up something of himself and of his own selfishness, and conduct himself with courtesy, with character and consideration—with forbearance, with faith and faithfulness.

* * *

"What therefore God hath joined together, let not man put asunder." [40]
—Jesus of Nazareth

When to Say It—and When to Be Silent

As was observed many centuries ago: There is "a time to every purpose . . ."[41] And there are times when some things should be said, and times to keep silent. There are times when we are tempted to make cutting comments, when the quality of kindness (and good sense itself) would suggest that we keep silent.

Sometimes on the football field we see the dangerous practice of "piling on"—piling on and pushing the bottom player a little farther down into the dirt. In life there is also the practice of "piling on" and pushing people down a little deeper—with words. Sometimes we see it among children. If one of them has made a misstatement or mistake, all present sometimes seem to want to outdo one another in embarrassing the unfortunate offender. But even as adults, too many of us, too often, are cutting in our comments and too sharp with our tongues. Too many of us correct others cruelly, with the wrong spirit, at the wrong time. Even in families, correction is often ill-timed; and the intended lesson may be lost by the resentment that comes with being embarrassed before others.

There are times to speak up; there are times to say what should be said. There are truths that must be spoken, falsehoods that must be challenged, misimpressions that must be corrected, and facts that must be made known. But the ill-timed lashing of an uncontrolled temper or a loose and irresponsible tongue can do irreparable damage. No friendship, no household, no marriage, no society is strong enough to remain unmarked by unbridled sarcasm or by cruel comment.

Whether uttered inadvertently or otherwise, we are responsible for the weight of our words, and we should weigh them well before we let them loose, having the good sense sometimes to be silent, and not to let temper or bad timing void the lessons that might have been learned. And on those occasions which must and do call for sharp correction, we should show "forth afterwards an increase of love toward him whom [we have] reproved," [42] for love can make correction lasting, but hate only hardens the human heart.

May God give us the good sense to know what to say, and when to say it, and when to be silent; and give us also the great quality of kindness so that what is said, will correct and not merely cruelly cut.

Quick-triggered Temper

It is written in the scriptural record that the Lord God gave man dominion over all the earth.[43] But subduing the earth loses much of its meaning unless we also subdue ourselves, our appetites, our anger.

In many respects the measure of a man is the measure of the things that make him angry. The striking without thinking, the hasty ill-timed act or utterance are all part of the measure of a man. As one physician said of himself: "My life is in the hands of any fool who makes me lose my temper." [44] But any fool who loses his temper takes not only his own life in his hands, but the lives of others also.

Those who, for example, drive in anger are a menace to all mankind. (It would be interesting to know, and appalling also, how many highway accidents have occurred because of anger, because of the hateful heated spirit of retaliation, the cutting in, the crowding over, despite all danger, to show people and put them in their place.) Injury and violent death in many forms are often the outcome of unreasoning anger, and a man who lets loose his quick-triggered temper with fists or weapons or words is likely to have a lifetime to regret his lack of self-control. He may sever a friendship; he may break a marriage; he may ruin a home; he may injure or destroy a life by his ill-timed temper.

No doubt all of us have been guilty of anger, and no doubt there *is* such a thing as righteous wrath—things we should be angry at. But blind, unreasoning anger can be a fury of destructive force—to ourselves and to others also. In the words of William Penn, "Every stroke our fury strikes is sure to hit ourselves at last." [45]

Suppose the Lord God were to strike out at us as we would strike out at someone else who happens to try our temper. If He should lash out at us as we are sometimes tempted to lash out at others, we should be chastened in a way we wouldn't forget—for surely most of us must have tried His patience many times.

There are those who would question, as a practical matter, the concept that the Saviour uttered in the Sermon on the Mount: that the "meek . . . shall inherit the earth." [46]—but to see peace and love and respect and so much else that is priceless and precious destroyed by unrighteous, unreasoning anger, gives much more meaning to the kind of meekness the Saviour must have had in mind. We shall never have a satisfactory dominion over ourselves or over anything else until we learn to control our tempers.

"A Woman Set Apart..."

In one account of the courtship of Elizabeth Barrett she replied to the importuning poet Robert Browning, that she should not marry because of her physical frailty; that if she should, as she poignantly put it, she would be "haunted by the ghosts of [his] unborn children." [47]

This thought has some searching meanings for this day. There are many avenues of activity open to this generation of young women. Indeed, there seem to be few that are closed to them. But in contemplating all of the open avenues, God grant that none who have given themselves in marriage and who are able, may be so shortsighted as to close their eyes to the career of hallowed motherhood.

There are less burdensome pursuits. There are avenues of more monetary remuneration, of more independence, more freedom, more convenience; of more glamour, perhaps, of a certain kind. But where is there one so richly rewarding, so fully satisfying, so assuredly consistent with the meaning and purpose of life, so close in companionship with God; so devoutly to be wished for, so earnestly to be prayed for, so completely to be accepted, as the career of virtuous, faithful motherhood in honorable marriage?

And this we would say to young mothers who find the days heavy, the evenings weary, the chores multiplied, the problems perplexing—but the rewards so wonderfully rich—this we would say to them, in some choice quoted sentences from the pages of the poets: "There will be a singing in your heart; there will be a rapture in your eyes; you will be a woman set apart; you will be so wonderful and wise." [48] And "Thou, while thy babes around thee cling, shalt show us how divine a thing a woman may be made." [49]

* * *

"For this cause shall a man leave his father and mother, and shall be joined unto his wife, and they two shall be one flesh." [50]

—Jesus of Nazareth

A Fresh Look at Life...

Sometimes it would be well if we could step aside and see ourselves as if we had never seen us before—and see not only ourselves, but see also the things around us, free from the tired impressions we have of places and people. Our thoughts, our very lives, often become imprisoned by the commonplace, by the familiar look of familiar things—things which if lost, would be wonderfully welcome if we should we find them once again.

It would be well to take a fresh new look not only at ourselves and our surroundings, but also to look at our loved ones, whom we sometimes so much take for granted. It would be well to take a fresh look at the loveliness of each new day; at the place we go when the day is done; at the walls we live within. The places we live in and the people we live with are not perfect (as we ourselves are not perfect). They may not always be at their best (as we ourselves are not always at our best). But it would be well at times to look at them as if we had lost them—and then suddenly saw them there.

So often we succumb to the commonplace. Much of boredom, of pessimism, much of discouragement, much of disinterest comes from thinking of familiar things in the same familiar way, of letting

[103]

our minds run in ruts, of thinking the same thoughts, thoughtlessly in the same sequence, instead of mentally stepping aside and seeing ourselves, our surroundings, our loved ones and our very lives with daily gratitude to God for all that is ours.

This world we live in is not a thing of chance; nor do we have a limitless lease on the life that here we live, nor on our loved ones in this life. And we are none too young to step aside and see ourselves in our own familiar setting, and ask what really matters most. And seen in proper perspective, the scramble for the shoddy things would seem shoddier; and life and loved ones, and work, and peace, and virtue, and a quiet conscience, and the beauty of the earth, and the sound and solid things would all take on new meaning. And somehow we would come closer to acquiring the courage to live as we should live and to be what we should be—if we would step aside and see ourselves and our surroundings with a new appraisal and purpose.

* * *

"Whatever woman may cast her lot with mine, should any ever do so, it is my intention to do all in my power to make her happy and contented; and there is nothing I can imagine that would make me more unhappy than to fail in the effort." [51]

—Abraham Lincoln

It's a Family Matter...

"There is little less trouble in governing
a private family than a whole kingdom." [52]
—Michel De Montaigne

On Living in Tight Compartments...

Sometimes some people seem to pride themselves on being self-contained, on withholding their thoughts and experiences from others. Up to a point, this may be evidence of a strong and admirable self-reliance. But the most enjoyed things in life are enjoyed as they are shared.

Consider, for example, the common, and often humorously referred to occurrence, of people's telling of their operations. Even that questionable enjoyment isn't what it might be unless there is someone else to tell it to. Trips taken are more enjoyed, first of all if there are others along, and secondly if there is someone to tell about them after they are over. Perhaps this explains in part the prevalent practice of bringing back pictures and insisting on showing them—even at the risk, sometimes, of being a bit boring. Life is much more satisfying with something shared.

Sometimes husbands and wives live too much within themselves, not sharing enough with one another: of thoughts, of hopes, even of fears, of heartfelt feelings, of pleasant things encountered during the day—in short, not enough of opening up, too much of living in tight compartments.

Sometimes children, too, live in tight compartments, and too closely keep their confidences from parents. (And sometimes parents are at fault in seeming to be too busy to listen!) Mothers and fathers and children are missing something preciously essential if they don't share sincerely, understandingly, with one another, something of the circle in which they live their separate lives.

There is strength and safety in sharing—even in sharing fears and troubles when there is need of it. Part of living consists of learning to be a good listener, and part consists of giving out, of entering into, of learning to share ourselves. And refraining from confidences with those we love and live with is not a very rewarding way of life.

It is a trite thing to say, a platitude concerning which there will be some cynicism, but it is true: that in sharing we receive, that in giving we get. And for a daughter or a son to come home of an evening and to tell of a lovely time makes the experience not only his again—but others' also.

To paraphrase one word of this deeply significant sentence from the Saviour: "For whosoever will save his life shall lose it: and whosoever will [share] his life . . . shall find it" [53]—over and over again.

On Keeping Confidences

As already observed, there is strength and safety and sincere satisfaction in sharing thoughts and feelings and experiences with those we love and live with—husbands and wives, children with parents, families sharing with one another something of their separate circles. There is strength and safety in the counsel and confidence of more than one mind, and both in times of happiness and in times of trouble we all need someone to confide in, someone to share with, someone to talk to.

(Of course, there is such a thing as being too talkative, too trivial, of telling too much too tiresomely. And there is such a thing also as being too intrusive in attempting to pry out confidences with insensitive insistence.) But all this aside, it is wonderfully reassuring and satisfying to have someone to be safe with, someone to trust, someone to talk to understandingly and openly—without holding ourselves too tightly; without the feeling that we must speak through narrow, guarded slits; without the fear of letting someone see inside.

Sometimes things don't come into focus until they are talked out, and in thinking out loud, in sharing confidences with someone who has a right to share them, counsel becomes wiser, safer, and more mature. One of the surpassing blessings of life is to have someone to listen, someone to understand, someone close and comfortable and trusted, with the assurance that what is said will be respected, not misunderstood, not distorted, not misquoted, not misused.

In some respects, "it is a greater compliment to be trusted than to be loved"—and to deserve to be trusted. And as we have a right to expect the confidences of those we love and live with, so we have an obligation to respect and keep such confidences— and never to let one who shares a confidence with us be embarrassed by it.

The essence of these thoughts has been beautifully phrased in this summarizing sentence: "Oh, the comfort, the inexpressible comfort, of feeling safe with a person, having neither to weigh thoughts, nor measure words—but pouring them all right out— just as they are—chaff and grain together—certain that a faithful hand will take and sift them—keep what is worth keeping—and with the breath of kindness blow the rest away." [55]

Someone to Be Safe with...

We have talked of sharing and of keeping confidences. Now, for a moment, we should like to talk of someone to trust—someone to be safe with. There are many exciting people, many talented and able and entertaining people, many charming and engaging people, who add interest and usefulness and color to any occasion. But beyond all this, among the greatest blessings of life is to feel safe with someone.

In many things we are very dependent upon other people. We don't have the knowledge or skill or ability to do some things for ourselves. And since this is so, it is a surpassing blessing to have someone to trust—someone to be safe with. But there is no real safety or peace or assurance with anyone without integrity, without high qualities of character.

It is a blessing and an obligation to see that our children are safe. Blessed is the child who can come with his hurts and his troubles to someone he can trust, and be enfolded in loving arms, with the blessed assurance of being safe with someone. And not only is it so with children, but with others also.

We likely wouldn't let an unknown, unbonded messenger carry large amounts of money from bank to bank. But do we assure ourselves how safe our loved ones are? Would we entrust a daughter, for example, to unknown and unproved companions. Is there anything more priceless than virtue? Than chastity? Would we leave priceless and irreplaceable things to chance? This is plain speaking—but not too plain for speaking of life and peace and safety and happiness, and of infinitely important and irreplaceable things.

Among the greatest blessings in life is to be safe with someone—someone without evil intent, someone who wouldn't violate a trust, who wouldn't take advantage of innocence or ignorance; someone who isn't planning in his heart to cut across conventions, to compromise principles, or to deprive another person of virtue, chastity, honor, or any priceless or irreplaceable possession. We may have all else in life, but if we can't count on character, on integrity, if we haven't the sense of being safe, we have little that matters very much. Oh the joy, the surpassing joy of having someone we can turn to, someone we can trust. "Oh, the comfort, the inexpressible comfort, of feeling safe with a person . . ."[55]

Parents Must Be Parents...

Young people often ask: "Why do parents worry so much, and watch us so closely, and repeat so often the same precautions? We are able to take care of ourselves. Why don't they leave us alone and let us learn in our own way?" In short, it seems that young people want to know why parents must act like parents!

The fact is that there is no acceptable way for parents to free themselves from parental responsibility. They have no choice if they do their duty before the law, before society, and before God. They must counsel; they must caution; they must be concerned; they must pass on to their children the benefit of their own experience and of others. In other words, they *must* act like parents— or be derelict in their duty.

This brings to mind the poignant comment of a girl who heard her companions complaining of their parents—complaining of being counseled and cautioned, of being asked where they were going, who they were going with, and of being told at what hour they should be in—to all of which she said: "You should be grateful to have someone think enough of you to care where you're going and when you will be back. My parents don't seem to care."

This sobered those who had joined in the general complaining.

Parents may send their children to school or into other supervised activities, and be physically free of them for a few hours, or even for many months—but still the primary responsibility for children must rest upon parents. Some parents will do their work better than others, some with more understanding, some with less irritation, some seemingly with less obvious intrusion. Some teachings might seem tiresome; some at times might even seem unessential—but parents must play the part of parents, and children must recognize the part that parents must play, and be willing to listen and learn. So far as parents and children are concerned, there is no honorable way by which they can free themselves from their continuing obligations to one another.

Occasions for Confidence

A s concerning young people, parents are sometimes heard to say: "I don't know what more
I can do. I have given them everything anyone
could ask." (But sometimes it seems that we are
willing to give everything—except ourselves!)

How many fathers, for example, are willing to
buy costly sports equipment—but don't take time
to use it with their boys? How many parents are
willing to buy their children the "best education"—
but don't take time to teach them some of the
precious things that aren't found in the catalogue
or the curriculum? How many parents are willing
to send their children to the country, to camp, or
almost anywhere—but feel a little too much relieved when they are out of the way? (How many
of us hope that they will get elsewhere what it is
our duty and privilege to give them at our own
knees?)

There are many agencies and organizations to
take over their time—but it isn't only a question of
keeping them otherwise occupied. There are some
things that come only by intimate association, only
by earnest understanding. And when a youngster
needs to talk out a personal problem, there isn't any
substitute for sitting down and giving the time it

[115]

takes to talk it out. And if we pass up the hour or evening when his heart is open for close confidences or when his arms are open for affection, who knows how much it might have meant!

These occasions of confidence, these times of teaching from the heart, these precious hours and evenings are perishable and priceless. And yet how many of us are doing almost everything else—and permitting them to pass? How many of us are taking time to talk to their hearts, to feed their souls with things that are beyond books, to make them feel that they can come to us with their most intimate confidences without fear of being brushed off or misunderstood.

There is more to being a good parent than providing physical necessities and arranging for formal instruction (important as these are). And beyond what we may be willing to buy them or where we may be willing to send them, we should ask ourselves if we are willing to sit down, and listen long, and take time to say some of those things that sometimes so much need to be said, and to live some of those hours that so much need to be lived with those who have close claims upon our lives and our love.

The Problem of Disciplining People...

There is an always urgent field for thought in the problem of disciplining people. Parents, and others, frequently find themselves searching and praying and pleading for wisdom and guidance in the teaching and disciplining of young and impressionable people (and of others also).

There has been a long-continuing controversy on the question of how harsh to be, how severe, how lax, how indulgent—a controversy that has seen the duty of discipline torn at times between the tendency to be too severe, too demanding, and the tendency to be too soft, too indifferent, too indulgent. Not only from one generation to another, but also perhaps from time to time in our own lives as individuals, we have seen the swaying between the old adage "Spare the rod and spoil the child" (which concept has often been abused), and the softer sound of simply "spoiling the child" (which has also been abused).

There is no known infallible formula for the problem of disciplining people. To prepare such a prescription for all circumstances and situations would seemingly require a wisdom exceeding that of Solomon. But in any such prescription, there are some essential component parts and some elements to be utterly avoided:

First of all, there should be no laxness or indifference to duty. There should be a fairness and consistency of penalties imposed, with a judicious weighing of facts. And, finally (and in punishment it may seem paradoxical), there should be love. Punishment in hate may leave its ugly, inerasable marks both upon the giver and the receiver. But punishment in love is likely to leave its lasting benefits without leaving marring marks—punishment that reproves "with sharpness" as occasion may require, and then shows forth "an increase of love toward him whom thou hast reproved, lest he esteem thee to be his enemy." [56] In the highest tradition of teaching and in the real work of making men, we can't lead a child, we can't lead anyone, very far without love. We can drive with hate, with threats, with fear, with force. But if we want a girl or boy to be his best, there must be a basis of love underlying all our actions and attitudes.

About Mothers...

One could search and ponder long without finding anything new to say concerning mothers. But need there be anything new? To say that there is nothing new is not to say that some things should not be said again. Appreciation, deserved praise, assurances of love need often be expressed—for either gratitude is a living thing, like music being heard, or it is a dead thing, like music that is heard no more. One cannot be long sustained by yesterday's song (nor yet live long on yesterday's nourishment). It is the song that now is being sung, the music that now is being heard, the strength that now sustains us, the gratitude that now we feel (and somehow now give evidence of) that is the living thing.

And as to mothers: gratitude for them is one of life's precious privileges—for there is no act of kindness, no hour of service, no loving thought, no office of hallowed motherhood that does not deserve acknowledgment in some sweet way—not always in audible utterance but in a loving gesture, a welcoming kiss, the sharing of a confidence, a little help, an understanding heart. These things, and much more, are the due of mothers—not for some far future time, but now while they are with us. Mother's Day is the reminder of some things that cannot be replaced or fully appraised or appreciated, and which can only partly be repaid by a gratitude that shows itself each day as a present, living part of life.

Is there nothing new about mothers? If not, neither is there anything new about spring, nor about love, nor about the goodness of life or of living. It isn't the newness of things that we need, but the solid, satisfying things that endure—like the love of mothers, like their service, like their sacrifices, like their willingness to give their lives that we might live; like their presence when we come home—like the emptiness we feel when they are no more there. Then we know that gratitude should be—always—a thing that somehow shows itself as a song that now is being sung.

For Fathers...

Much of life is made up of things we think we will one day do: of things we postpone, of things we set aside, of things we leave too late. And one of the things we could best determine to do this day, would be for fathers and sons (and daughters) to draw a little nearer, to come a little closer—to take a little more time for a closer kind of companionship with those who mean the most.

Too many of us wait too long for the cherished times together, for the intimate outings, for the quiet hours of an evening, for the fuller talking out of important personal problems with the close confidence of an understanding heart. It is not so much the sending; it is not so much the preaching of the precepts; it is not altogether, even, the providing— but the going with, the doing with, the being with that brings a closer kind of kinship.

Fathers are often too closely confined to the business of providing things physical and financial. Often in their daily pursuits, they live competitive lives to make the means to help to make the home— to provide the things by which their loved ones may better live. And being preoccupied with pressure and problems, they may sometimes leave some things too late.

One day all of us, alike, will stand before the Father of us all, to give an account of what we have done with what we have had. And when that day comes for all of us, God grant that, through the useful virtue of our lives, we shall be an honor to the "fathers of our flesh," [57] as well as to "the Father of [our] spirits" [57]—that we shall be such sons and daughters that He could say also of us: "This is my beloved Son, in whom I am well pleased." [58]

God bless the fathers who have faced the world for us in many ways, and grant that there may be a closer kind of companionship between fathers and daughters and sons—that fathers may have a fuller sense of being fathers, and that sons may have a finer sense of being sons—and that both may seek to see and do the things for one another that are sometimes left too late.

In Turning Homeward...

There is something hallowed in turning homeward. Homeward turns the child tired from school or play. Homeward turns the man or woman weary from work, weary from the problems and the hard competitive pace. Homeward turn the tired to the long shadows of the sunset. "All things turn home at eventide."

Home—and Mother—and Memories: memories of turning home when hungry; of turning home when cold, when hurt, when sick; of turning home when the rough abrasive side of the world has rubbed us roughly; of turning home when happy; and of turning home when there is nowhere else to turn—home, to an open door, to a sense of belonging, to a sense of safety and assurance! Home—and Mother—and Memories!

But as to young mothers: they hardly have time for memories. What they need are more hands, more hours, more help; and it seems that there should be at least two of themselves to be all that they are, as small hands pull at their skirts, as small arms reach out for them. They are so very much wanted, so very much a part of everything.

But think for a moment what it would mean to be the center of so much, to be so much sought and consulted; to be the very queen of a family circle; to be looked to for almost everything, in the midst of demanding noises, sometimes tiring noises, but nevertheless of meaningful and wonderful noises— to be the center of all this, and then suddenly to have it all cease. Think what it would mean to feel needed so much, and then to feel needed no more; to have those with whom we have shared so much move out and take their interests elsewhere. And then—think what it would mean to be remembered!

This brings us once more to the subject of sharing—not only the sharing of our substance, but also the sharing of our very selves, our thoughtfulness, our love, with those who have shared so much with us. For this day—and for others also—let there be a kind of kindly sharing; a sharing of the time it takes to go home, to call home, to write home; to remember those who are there, even though other obligations have taken us somewhat from their close and constant circle. Let there be some message, some gesture of remembrance, some sharing of confidence, some sharing of ourselves, some sharing of our lives with other lonely lives. And let there be no lonely unremembered mothers.

There is something hallowed in turning homeward . . .

"All Present or Accounted for..."

It is a wonderful, comforting, reassuring feeling when parents, mentally, can call the roll, and find all the family in—safe and secure. When families are young in years, it is comparatively easy to feel assured that they are somewhat safe, or at least to be assured that they are all in. But when they grow older, and their interests and activities widen, and they become more independent the waiting hours of night are often long, as they come home, one by one.

Sometimes children, young and old, wonder why parents worry so much and are so concerned about their unaccounted absences. But both caution and concern come with experience and responsibility—and not without reason. There are so many hazards, so many things that could and have happened, and parents cannot, or should not, escape an acute sense of concern for all who are not present or accounted for.

Children should and must expect to keep parents informed of their absences and activities. It isn't good for anyone of any age to be unaccounted for. Otherwise an unexplained absence or accident or illness could go unknown and undetected for far too long a time. Apart from love, apart from parental responsibility, it is simply a matter of good sense and safety for someone who has an interest in us to know always and at all hours, where we are, with whom we are, where we can be reached, and when we are expected to arrive. Less accountability than this, less responsibility, is much too loose. And in these matters, youth should not and must not think that parents are prying. It's just that they need to know, for theirs is an inescapable obligation which they cannot set aside if they would and should not if they could.

This sure sense of responsibility is suggested in the Saviour's parable of the shepherd and the sheep: "What man of you, having an hundred sheep, if he lose one of them, doth not leave the ninety and nine . . . and go after that which is lost, until he find it? And when he hath found it, he layeth it on his shoulders, rejoicing. And when he cometh home, he calleth together his friends and neighbours, saying unto them, Rejoice with me; for I have found my sheep which was lost." [59]

It is a blessed thing, in the hours of the night, and at all other hours also, to have the sweet assurance that all are "present or accounted for," and we owe it, all of us, to all of us, to see that it is so.

* * *

"The happiest moments of my life have been the few which I have passed at home in the bosom of my family." [60]
—Thomas Jefferson

Some Plain Talk on Teaching

"Take heed lest by any means this liberty of yours become a stumblingblock to them that are weak." [61]

—Paul the Apostle

On Influencing Others

Fashion is one evidence of the influence people have on other people. Just who sets the subleties of fashion is difficult to say, but, as Benjamin Franklin observed: It seems that there are those "who, perhaps, fear less the being in hell than out of fashion" [62]—and there is little reason to suppose that this feeling is strictly confined to the feminine part of the population. We all tend to follow custom more or less, to follow traditional ways. And in part at least, we also tend to follow changing fashion.

There may be some unusually independent people who feel that they aren't influenced by the example of others, but all of us are influenced more than we think. And often the new things we think we need, we think we need not so much because the old ones are worn out, but because they are out of fashion. As Shakespeare said: "The fashion wears out more apparel than the man." [63]

But fashion is just one way in which we are influenced by others. And as we are influenced by others, so also we influence others, whether we know it or not. And as we influence them, so we are responsible for the effect of our influence, whether we know it or not. We have an inescapable responsibility for the example we set and for the opinions we express before people, especially before young and impressionable people. The child who hears us make a remark, cannot always distinguish between what we are stating as unassailable truth and what we are stating purely as theory or supposition or personal opinion—or even as sarcasm, when we say one thing and mean the absolute opposite.

Every person, however inconspicuous, has his weight with others, and is (in this sense, as in others also), his brother's keeper. Every child, every man, every woman, is being made and molded by what he hears, what he sees, what he senses in the acts and utterances and attitudes of others. Every writer, every teacher, every speaker, every friend and companion—indeed every person—is responsible for his effect on others, whether his relationships are professional or personal.

As we touch the lives and minds of other men, we would well remember the words of Paul: "Take heed lest by any means this liberty of yours become a stumblingblock to them that are weak." [64] —or we might add, lest it become a stumblingblock to anyone at all—weak or strong—for the lives of all of us are vitally affected by the attitudes and ideas and actions and utterances of all of us. And we can no more let ideas loose without responsibility than we can let germs loose without responsibility.

"And They Shall Teach Their Children..."

O ne of the most moving scenes of sacred writ is the one wherein the Saviour said, "Suffer little children, and forbid them not, to come unto me: for of such is the kingdom of heaven." [65] This, coupled with an earlier utterance, suggests the sweetness and cleanness with which children come here from the presence of the Father: "And Jesus called a little child unto him, and set him in the midst of them, And said, Verily I say unto you, except ye be converted, and become as little children, ye shall not enter into the kingdom of heaven." [66] And then He added a sentence that suggests the weight of responsibility that the presence of children imposes upon us, and which suggests also the gravity of the offense of destroying faith: "But whoso shall offend one of these little ones which believe in me, it were better for him that a millstone were hanged about his neck, and that he were drowned in the depth of the sea." [67]

In a well-known work of literature, Prince Myshkin had this sentence to say: "The soul is healed by being with children." [68] Healed, yes—and also searched. Perhaps we are never more open to searching scrutiny than when the eyes of a child are upon us. And so often we underestimate their understanding. As Emerson observed, "[Boys] know truth from counterfeit as quick as the chemist does. They detect weakness in your eye and behavior . . . before you open your mouth . . ." [69] Don't try to hide your heart from a child.

Children have a way of seeing inside. And our teaching must be more than talking. We must be careful what they feel from us, what they see inside us, besides the things we say. They come here clean and sweet and teachable, from the Father of us all, and we have an inescapable obligation to teach and train them early, and not to leave their teaching to chance: to teach them reverence and righteousness and respect, honor and obedience; to teach them faith, to teach them truth.

"And again, inasmuch as parents have children in Zion, . . . that teach them not to understand . . . the sin be upon the heads of the parents." [70] "And they shall also teach their children to pray, and to walk uprightly before the Lord." [70] "I have commanded you to bring up your children in light and truth . . ." [71] And "whoso shall offend one of these little ones which believe in me, it were better for him that . . . he were drowned in the depth of the sea." [67]

Such is the inescapable obligation imposed by the presence of children, and such is the gravity of the offense of destroying faith—in children, in youth, or, for that matter, in anyone at all.

Not from Fear...

There are many factors that go into the making of men; and some, such as fear and love, are as different as light and darkness. There is a question as to just how much fear can do in the making of a man. The fear of want may make him work a little harder or, save a little more, but it is doubtful that fear alone will ever make a man amount to very much.

And it is doubtful if you can frighten a man into being good—basically, inwardly, willingly good— any more than you can legislate a man into being good. The law is always there. The actual or potential punishments and penalties are always in evidence, but men still engage in all manner of malpractice, despite the fear of penalties and punishments.

A child who is afraid of his parents may put forth some constructive effort to please or placate them, but he doesn't develop into the man he might be simply from being afraid.

Fear may prevent some things, indeed, many things. And it may be the spur for some kinds of accomplishment. But to be at his best, to do his best, to develop his best, a man must be running after something rather than merely running away from

something. He must have the incentive to succeed—
and not merely the fear of failure. Thus the posi-
tive approach to teaching is the one most richly
rewarding, with hope, encouragement, love, incentive and assurance.

Life is an opportunity. It is limitless and everlasting, and happiness is the end and object of it,
here and hereafter. To hold out to a man the assurance of eternal life, of everlasting association
with those he loves, of limitless and everlasting
progress and possibilities, combined with peace and
a quiet conscience and an inner sense of approval
in the present—all these offer so much more to work
for than simply the fear of falling short. And we
should live good lives, not from the fear of what
will happen if we don't, but for the joy of what will
happen as we do—because keeping the commandments God has given, gives peace, happiness, good
appetite, good conscience, and a wonderful assurance of moving toward the great and good goal that
a loving Father has placed within the reach of each
of us.

We should be what we should be and go where
we should go and do what we should do, not from
fear, but because that way leads to happiness and
peace and progress.

Freedom and Force

There is no more basic question in life than the question of freedom and force. No doubt it was a foremost question before the world was. If there is to be order, there must be law. But with freedom there is always likely to be some violation of law. And so there must be some enforcement, and enforcement implies penalties and punishment (as well as rewards). And penalties and punishment imply some curtailment of freedom and perhaps some use of physical force. And if there are things we are prevented from doing, how much freedom have we? As youngsters sometimes ask: "Do I *have* to do it? If freedom is an inalienable right, why can't I do what I want to do?"

These aren't easy questions to answer in an absolute sense, for despite our universal likenesses, there are innumerable differences, in people and personalities and in situations and circumstances. Perhaps there isn't any unfailing formula—and that there was once a war in heaven would seem to be the evidence of it. But part of the answer to the question of how much freedom we have is this: Uninhibited freedom stops where it infringes on the freedom of others. Another part of the answer is that abuse of freedom may lead to its loss.

Teaching people to want to do what they ought to do is one way to a fuller freedom. Nor even is this unfailingly easy. Children can usually be led with love, kindness, patience, persuasion, reason. But with children (as well as with adults) some measure of authority and physical force cannot always be avoided. But the mere fact that we have the authority and the power to do a thing doesn't mean that the best way of doing it is by physical force. Far from it—for whenever a situation deteriorates into the use of force and force alone, it is evidence that someone, somehow, somewhere has tragically failed, and that we have lost something that we cannot afford to lose. To quote in closing:

> Know this, that every soul is free
>   To choose his life and what he'll be,
> For this eternal truth is given
>   That God will force no man to heaven.
>
> He'll call, persuade, direct aright,
>   And bless with wisdom, love, and light,
> In nameless ways be good and kind,
>   But never force the human mind.[72]
>   —William C. Gregg

The Liability of Loose Threats

Sometimes someone is heard to say what he will do to someone else—if—! And in that "if" a threat is uttered or implied. Threats may seem necessary under some circumstances, but all of us under all circumstances should be scrupulously cautious concerning our intentions against others, because a threat is a challenge, a dare in a sense; and, human nature being what it is, threats often have exactly the opposite effect of what was intended.

There are many ways of threatening: Words are one way; attitudes and innuendo are another; weapons are another. A threatening gun, even an empty gun, has often proved to be a source of trouble and tragedy, by the sheer suggestion of intention to intimidate. If a person points a gun or shows one, or even if he has one, by his very pointing or possession he says in effect that he will shoot under some circumstances—else why would he have one? And the person who is threatened cannot be expected to know how earnest is the actual intent. (We never know quite how far to believe a bluff.)

Any evidence of evil or adverse intent is a threat. A clenched fist is a threat. It implies that it will be used if—if certain conditions are not complied with, just as a gun implies that it will be used if—if, for example, the bank cashier doesn't hand the cash over the counter as commanded. And so it must follow that a threat is presumed to be punishable because it is evidence of intent. As a man thinketh, so is he, and as he threatens, so must he expect to be held accountable.

The question of threatening is particularly important in dealing with children, for children soon learn to know whether or not we are earnest in our intent, whether or not we will do what we say we will do. And if they find that our threats are empty, our influence and authority are weakened with them. On the other hand if we threaten unjustly, or if in anger we threaten more than the circumstances suggest, and then follow through our unjust threat, then we lose face and faith and love and confidence—and maybe much more. Perhaps it would be too extreme to say that we should never threaten, but it is certainly not too extreme to say that a loose threat is a liability, for we are accountable for our intentions as well as for our actions and utterances.

A Favor for Ourselves

We often see the familiar picture of parents and teachers pleading with young people to improve themselves, to learn their lessons, to make the most of their lives. And because of this sincere anxiety on the part of parents, young people may sometimes assume that they are doing teachers or parents a favor by learning their lessons, by improving their lives.

In one sense this is true. It is true that much of the measure of a parent's success and satisfaction is found in the soundness and happiness and success of his children. It is true that much of a teacher's success is found in the lessons that his students learn. But in another sense, it is a peculiar paradox that parents or teachers should so much, so long, so patiently have to plead with young people to make good use of their lives—for every effort they make, all the knowledge they acquire, every lesson they learn is for their own everlasting advantage. And in doing what they should do and in learning what they should learn, they are doing a favor for themselves.

Leaving for the moment the matter of prodding and persuading young people, may we look briefly at another side of the subject: Sometimes we may think that we have done someone else a special favor if we live according to law. Sometimes we may think we are doing the Lord God a special favor if we keep His commandments. And it is true that it would please Him to have us do so, for His declared purpose is to bring to pass the happiness and peace and everlasting progress of His children. For this cause were the commandments given, and for this cause He has patiently repeated them through His servants the prophets. But in keeping them, we serve first ourselves—no matter what we may do for others besides ourselves. And in breaking them we do injury to ourselves, no matter what we may do to others besides ourselves.

It is a great virtue to love and to please parents; it is a sincere satisfaction to a teacher to see a lesson learned; and it is good to keep the commandments for the approving favor of our heavenly Father. But in all this pleasing of others, in all this learning of lessons, in all this keeping of commandments, we do immeasurable service for ourselves. And others shouldn't have to plead with us so much or labor with us so long to persuade us to do what we ought to be anxiously doing as a favor for ourselves.

Men in the Making

As we see a new home, finished and landscaped and lovely, we may partly forget the process by which it was brought into being. There was dirt to be dug; and rough materials to be shaped and put in place—and littered plaster and sawdust and shavings and much noise along with all else. And while it was in the making, we had to have perspective, and we had to have faith: faith in the plan, in the blueprint, in the materials, and in the men who made it. We had to believe that it would someday be what it promised to be.

This is true of other things also. Paintings and portraits look anything but lovely when the artist first begins to daub. The pottery we see and buy and much admire begins as mud—a special kind of mud to be sure, but mud nevertheless.

When we see a boy in adolescence, or a boy first learning to play the piano, or a girl first fingering the violin, we have to have faith. The first hesitant notes, the first unsure sounds are not the finished product, but they are the promise of things to come. They are part of the practice and the pain that it takes to arrive at a finished performance. We need to know the ultimate objective and then trust people and principles and proven processes to bring about the ultimate outcome.

We have to trust for many things—intelligently—but we have to trust. And we have to overlook the imperfections of many things in the making. We are not perfect, any of us; and to others and to our Father in heaven we must look like pretty crude clay at times in some of our actions and utterances—and perhaps all of us have reason to criticize all of us in the eternal process of reaching for perfection. But if a person shows honest and earnest effort and intent to pursue sound purposes and principles, we should be as long-suffering (or try to be) as our Father in heaven is with us, and not be too quick to judge or criticize or condemn before we see the product in patient perspective.

Concerning Unproved Suppositions...

As young people face their formal education, there may be many puzzling questions that present themselves, some of which concern the constant discovery of new knowledge, some of which concern the flux and shiftings of conflicting theories. The past century or so has seen a profound unfoldment of truth, and the mind of man has been permitted by the Almighty to penetrate further in some fields than in several centuries preceding. But the past century or so has also seen much unprovable or unproved speculation, with some suppositions that have lacked sound substance.

Theories come and go, and dogmatism for any tentative concept, academic or otherwise, ill becomes anyone. And of those who are dogmatic in teaching popular but unproved opinions—indeed, of all of us—let these questions be asked: Who knows of a textbook that will not be revised? Who knows of a process that will not be improved? Who knows of a theory that is not subject to further findings? Who knows what holds the universe together—or even the smallest particle of it? Who knows what keeps it in its course?

[143]

We may have found some of the factors and forces, but we know so much less than all there is to know. And with the most learned often disagreeing with the most learned, to the student facing an overwhelming flood of facts and of alleged facts, it would be wise to say: Respectfully consider what is in the books; respectfully consider what is presented in the classroom—and respectfully reserve judgment where teachings come in conflict with other teachings.

There is so much that all of us together do not know. There is so much of supposition, of opinion, so much that is subject to further finding. But fortunately there are some great unchanging truths in the universe, and He who keeps creation in its course is the Source of them all. And we need not be unsettled by the shifting theories until the theories themselves are settled; until the conflicts are composed; until men know much more than they know now. In the meantime, we can search and seek, and cling to the great truth that truth does not come in conflict with truth.

With an open mind to truth, we shall someday know the answers that we so much seek. And until we know, we can walk confidently, humbly into the future—with faith.

"And Ye Shall Know the Truth..."

Not too infrequently it would be well to turn our attention to Pilate's timeless question, "What is truth?" [73]—for on the answer hangs all we are or ever hope to be. On the answer hangs our health and happiness, our peace and purpose, and the very issues of life and death, the very meaning of time and eternity. (We can never be assured of health or happiness or peace or settled purpose, unless we face the facts, the truth, about ourselves, our very nature, and about the things we should or shouldn't partake of and the things we should or shouldn't do.)

"What is truth?" It has been variously defined. Shakespeare said of it: "Truth is truth to the end of reckoning." [74] which is very like another definition that denotes truth as the absolute opposite of things changing and transitory: "Truth is knowledge of things as they are, and as they were, and as they are to come." [75] Of this we may be sure: Truth doesn't depend upon the theories and opinions of people. If men are in error, and if we follow them in their errors, that won't change truth. Socrates suggested this when he said: "If you will be persuaded by me, pay little attention to Socrates, but much more to the truth." [76]

Some fear the truth. Some have reason to. Some suppose it to be dangerous, frightening, uncomfortable—and often it is. Truth is so dangerous it sometimes makes martyrs of men. And surely it is dangerous and fatal to falsehood. It is dangerous and disturbing to complacency, to lazy thinking. It is disturbing to minds that are too comfortably closed. And because it is dangerous and disturbing there are always some who would suppress it and some who would dispense it sparingly. But disturbing or not, we are faced with this fact: Truth is never so dangerous as falsehood, never so dangerous as error, never so dangerous as deceit, and not nearly so dangerous as ignorance is.

Perhaps the most satisfying utterance of all time as to truth is this sentence from our Lord and Saviour: "And ye shall know the truth, and the truth shall make you free." [77] With this kind of counsel we cannot safely do other than seek the truth wherever it is, wherever it leads. Theories come and go. Popular opinions prevail for awhile. Fashions have their cycles, and conflicting ideas have their seasons of acceptance—but "the spirit of truth is of God" [78] and "abideth forever" [78] "and hath no end." [78] God help us to seek, to see, to say, to accept, to live by the truth, and find it wherever it is and follow it where it takes us—for it is not nearly so dangerous as ignorance is.

The Coming of Commencement

The coming of each commencement calls to mind the passing of another year so swiftly and so soon—and suggests once more to all of us that we ought to start early to do what we ought to be doing. A student cannot always soon decide what he may wish to do for all the rest of his life, but even if he hasn't decided on a final pursuit, he can always have some good goal in sight and be preparing himself for something sound and solid. No road leads nowhere, and no beginning goes nowhere. And just because we haven't decided what we want to be, is no reason why we should act as if we weren't going to be anything! In other words, we ought to be on our way.

Another thought that comes at commencement is this: that no one, young or old, should ever leave learning behind. No matter what classes we complete, no matter what degrees we acquire, no matter what school doors we walk out of, no matter what occupations we walk into, we should always keep an earnest and active interest in the world we live in, in the people we live with and in all the best of what is now known and in what will yet be discovered and revealed and made known.

The world is not static. Processes are constantly

improved. Discovery is ever adding and revealing heretofore unknown knowledge, and anyone who, leaving school, leaves also learning behind, will find himself farther and farther behind—for the destiny of man is limitless and everlasting. "Whatever principle of intelligence we attain unto in this life, it will rise with us in the resurrection." [79] And the more a man learns of truth, the better prepared he will be here, and the better prepared he will be hereafter—if conceit of learning doesn't lead him into stubborn error and false philosophies.

This brings us to a final comment on commencement: No matter how much we know, no matter what credits we acquire, no matter what courses we complete, what we know is an infinitely small part of all there is to know. Textbooks will change; theories will be set aside; processes will be improved—and we should keep our minds open to truth, free for the search, with humility before Him who gave us life, who reveals all truth, and who keeps creation in its course. Humility is especially becoming at commencement.

* * *

"A teacher affects eternity; he can never tell where his influence stops." [80]
—Henry Brooks Adams

To Youth Looking for a Future...

". . . Youth will always begin at the beginning . . ." [81]

—Goethe

The Weight of the Future...

Most of us at times feel overpowered and depressed by the tasks that lie before us, by the undone things that we have yet to do. A young man, for example, may look ahead at what he feels he must accomplish before he can feel somewhat settled: the years of school that are required; the time it takes for special preparation; the possibility of military service; the matter of marriage and the making of a home. And the time, the money, the effort and the years ahead may all seem to weigh on him at once.

Many of us have been through it. It is almost as if a man should look at a mortgage, and feel somehow that he has to pay it all right now instead of meeting it monthly. It is almost as if a mother should look at the mountains of meals she must prepare in a long lifetime, and feel that she must plan and prepare them all at once. But fortunately life is lived a day at a time. And while we must plan and prepare and earnestly move toward our ultimate objectives, the obligations of the future need not weigh us down as if they were all due and payable today. Indeed, if we were to let all future requirements worry and weigh upon us as if they were all due today, our present effectiveness would be impaired to the point where we would be less able to do what *is* due today.

To you, young man, looking forward with a long future before you: don't let it weigh on you as if you had to carry all its weight at once. Do well now what should now be done, and as the past has brought you to this point, so the future will take you further. You can't complete the whole curriculum in one week of worrying, nor even in one year of working. You can't take final steps until you have completed the prerequisites. And don't let the process become needlessly and painfully congested by trying to force too much of the future through channels that were made for present capacity.

To look ahead at the whole load and try to carry the weight of it all at once could depress and discourage and defeat any of us. With faith and work we may move the mountain in parts and in pieces. And with faith and work we can meet the obligations and opportunities of life by looking at the years ahead as a load that can be lifted a little at a time and not as one that weighs upon us all at once.

Keeping up . . .
and Catching up

We recall the often quoted comment of Lewis Carroll's Red Queen: "Now here, you see, it takes all the running you can do to keep in the same place." [82] It does require an earnest effort to keep even with life—and one of life's most discouraging experiences is to be always behind. Leaving things that might be done sooner, until just a little later, is a factor of unhappiness and failure.

This is evident in students who habitually leave homework too late and first pursue other pastimes and pleasures, and count on doing the essential things second—who ignore the alarm just a little too long, who leave home just a little too late, and who, literally or figuratively, live life breathlessly trying to beat the bell—and seldom arrive in time to be quite comfortable, or to seem settled or to feel prepared.

In the words of a wise educator: "It is easier to keep up than to catch up." [83] Cramming isn't a pleasant pursuit. Nor is trying to do several days' work in one. Loafing along and then trying to pour in, in one night, all the knowledge that should have been absorbed in small daily doses is always difficult and discouraging.

This is true not only of young people, not only of academic obligations, but in all of life's many other matters: Leaving to the end of the year what should be kept up currently, leaving too late any obligation of life, is an uncomfortable way of living, and is hazardous as to the things both of time and eternity. There is seldom any real reason to suppose that what we ought to be doing now will be easier to do after we find ourselves farther behind. There is seldom any experience to suggest that "sluffing" today and doubling the obligations of tomorrow will improve our future prospects.

To concur with the comment of the Red Queen: We have to run so fast to stay where we are. And to the student near the starting of school, and to all people at any point in life: "It is easier to keep up than to catch up." There is no better time to keep up than currently, and there is little reason to suppose that it will be easier to do all at once what should be done in digestible amounts each day.

Repentance is a great and blessed principle (one that all of us have need of), and catching up is a kind of repentance. But better than repentance is keeping the commandments; and better than catching up is keeping up—so that postponement and procrastination are not permitted to put an always uncomfortable penalty upon us.

The Spirit of "Getting by"...

There is a spirit that blights and shrivels the human soul whenever it remains unchallenged and unchecked. For want of better words, perhaps it could be called "the spirit of getting by"—of doing as little as possible, of giving as little as possible, of working as little as possible.

With young people in school it is sometimes manifest in an attitude of cutting corners and simply slipping through: in making a minimum effort to stay with the class; in studying as little as possible to acquire credit for the course; in being satisfied with a minimum passing mark without reaching out for the further knowledge that could be had with a little extra effort. Young people often seem to suppose that there is ample time in the far future for all that ought to be done, and that it is smart for the present simply to get by. And sometimes very late they learn that the days of this life are limited—sometimes so late that they may not see it until they have passed the peak and are looking down the other side of life.

But it isn't only among young people that this spirit has spread. Its infection is felt much farther and is manifest among men in many ways. While the spirit of getting by, of slipping through, the spirit of working little and giving less may sometimes seem smart and popular and approved, there is a law that says that benefits and blessings are predicated upon performance. We only grow by growing; we only do by doing—and he who shows a niggardly, unwilling nature, he who refuses to grow as much as he should grow, to learn as much as he should learn, to work as well as he could work —he who holds back his best efforts, whatever he may be doing to others, is cheating first himself, and dwarfing himself inside.

Quite safely it may be said: He who is afraid of doing too much, seldom does enough. "There is a law, irrevocably decreed . . . upon which all blessings [and benefits] are predicated," [84] and the spirit of slipping through, the spirit of simply getting by, will rob us of the richest rewards.

"Sitting This One Out..."

Sometimes too much of what we do—or think we do—is in the nature of simply sitting and seeing someone else do something. It is good to watch, to listen, to appreciate as others perform, but it is also essential to perform somewhat for ourselves. It is one of the irrevocable laws of life that we improve our power to do only by putting in the effort—only by practicing and performing.

Parents may be willing to do almost anything for their children. But there are some things that even parents cannot do for their children, no matter how much they may wish to. They can expose them to beneficial influences; they can set before them a proper example; they can send them to school; they can provide the encouragement, the atmosphere and the opportunities, but parents cannot learn their children's lessons for them, and they cannot acquire the skills for them. They can provide them, for example, the opportunity to take music lessons, but they cannot *give* them the art of playing or performing. That comes with a price, with practice, with some pain—with participation.

No doubt the Lord God could relieve us of the effort of life, as He could send manna from heaven. But if we didn't do some things for ourselves, we should never reach our highest possibilities. In a very real and ultimate sense, no one else can make of us what we will not pay the price of becoming. There are some things no one can make of us without our willingness, without our work.

And as to "sitting this one out," let it be said to young people especially: Sooner or later in life there comes a time when it is performance that counts—not promises, not possibilities, not potentialities—but performance. Sooner or later there comes a time when sitting and watching are not enough—when doing something for ourselves and doing something for others is essential. It is good to sit and listen; it is good to sit and watch; it is good to sit and learn. But the law of improvement is the law of practice, of participation, of performance.

It is all right to "sit out" some things, but it is tragic to sit out life and let it pass as if we were not a part of the picture.

"Marking Time..."

There are many circumstances and situations in which we may feel that we are marking time—or worse—wasting time. There are times when we are waiting for people and appointments when we feel cheated as we think of what we might have done with the time we waste in waiting. There are times of routine travel, of commuting between places when the interval may seem more or less lost.

There are times when we are pressed into pursuits not of our own choosing, on detours from our intended destination—as, for example, time spent in making a living at uninteresting routine work while waiting for other work, or while preparing for other pursuits, or time spent by young men in military service when they are eager to settle down to other purposes.

In these unavoidable interruptions, there is often much more that can be salvaged than is sometimes supposed. Wherever a man is, he has his mind with him. Wherever he is, he can think and plan and pursue, mentally at least, constructive purposes. Almost wherever he is he can arrange to read—not trash or trivia, but from the best books. It isn't always so, but it can often be so. Almost wherever a man is, he can write. It takes only simple tools to write—and some significant writings have come even from within prison walls. Some interesting and profitable activities have been pursued from the bedsides of shut-ins, by those who couldn't go out from where they were but who have reached out with what they had, with some wonderfully useful results.

A man can be immobilized without immobilizing his mind. Some of the most successful people have learned what to do with odd moments, with the in-between times that so many of us waste—sometimes just sitting, sometimes just waiting, sometimes with impatient pacing. Almost wherever a person is he can find some constructive purpose to pursue, without wasting time in shoddy or trivial or tawdry pursuits.

In a sense we can't "save" time as we can save water that would otherwise run away. But often when we are diverted from our intended course, we can make time serve as water that runs into a reservoir—a reservoir of preparation, of stored knowledge, of acquired skills—to be used for a better purpose at a better time and place rather than let it run away.

The Question of Quitting

Besides the more or less "normal" reasons for restlessness, we are all well aware of the added causes of uncertainty and indecision that confront our young people and of the reasons they have to wonder what they should do as they face an uncertain future. Of course, every generation sees the difficulties of its own day, and in an unsettled situation it is sometimes difficult to decide whether or not to return to school and settle down to serious studies. Often the very air and atmosphere seems to suggest giving up prolonged preparation and satisfying immediate demands. But one of the great lessons of life is to learn to appreciate the privileges of the present and to have faith in the future. And one of the great characteristics of youth is to have the courage and the faith to face the future with faith.

But sometimes young people quit without real cause to quit. Sometimes they quit from sheer restlessness. Sometimes they feel that they must have more money—and they quit to "work awhile." Sometimes they think they will stay out "only this one year." And sometimes they sacrifice permanent possibilities for immediate demands.

Time goes so quickly, and a year in which one

simply succumbs to restlessness is a lost year. Every unessential interruption breaks the pattern and habit of study and adds a penalty to preparation.

Of course when the calls of country come they must be met, but beyond essential calls may we suggest to you who are young: that you settle down and make the most of your period of preparation despite difficulty and discouragement, and prepare as far as you can for the long pull of life and let no superficial or unessential interruption dissuade you from your serious pursuits—for no matter what the future may hold, the best prepared people will be the best prepared to meet it.

Beyond the sincerely essential interruptions, the best thing you can do for yourself, your country, your family, and your future is to settle down and pursue permanent and worth-while purposes and make yourself as capable and competent as you can.

Do We Have Our Freedom?

Perhaps all of us at times have questions concerning freedom—especially young people who feel too closely tied, too closely tethered, and who sometimes seem to feel that freedom should mean the right to do absolutely anything they choose to do. Perhaps we have all heard youngsters say in substance: If it's a free country, why do I have to do anything I don't want to do? Why do I have to practice? Why do I have to go to school? Why do I have to come in early—or account to anyone at all? If it's a free country, why can't I go where I want and do what I want and take what I want?

Sooner or later, such misconceptions concerning freedom would, if persistently pursued, lead to loss of freedom. Absolute and unrestrained freedom is, of course, anarchy. And anarchy is not freedom, but complete chaos. We cannot have freedom without responsibility. We cannot have freedom without respecting the rights of others. We cannot have freedom without living within the law.

And as to young people who earnestly ask such searching questions concerning freedom, it may be helpful to remember these few simple essentials: Yes, we have our freedom—freedom to be lazy, freedom to refuse to work, freedom to refuse to take

[163]

advantage of our opportunities (even freedom to starve if we want to); freedom to be dishonest, freedom to be unpleasant, unkind, unco-operative; freedom to choose right or wrong, honesty or dishonesty, chastity or unchastity, industry or indolence, honor or dishonor, truth or falsehood, good or evil, light or darkness, the wrong road or the right one. In all this we have our choice, but in all of this also there is one thing we must remember: there is no such thing as freedom from consequences.

Freedom is a God-given inalienable right, and is essential to the soul's salvation in the highest sense. And every man must be protected in his right to choose as to certain essentials. But, when we flaunt any law—of society, of the land, of nature, or of God—we pay a price. We reap the results of the seeds we sow. Freedom can be used or abused, but there is this certainty concerning it: it cannot keep us from consequences.

How to Behave Away from Home

For school and work and for other purposes many young people find themselves away from home, some for the first time. And not only with young people, but with others also, the problem of how to behave away from home is a persistent problem. But it shouldn't be a particularly perplexing problem because a person is what he is wherever he is. Principles don't change with geography.

But sometimes people suppose that there is a different code of conduct away from home, and that they can count on not being known. This might be true in fiction, but it isn't true in fact. In fiction and in fairy tale a favorite plot is for the prince to move among his people in disguise. Such plots have a host of variations in a long line of literature, and it makes exciting reading when the pauper proves to be the prince or when the grand lady changes places with her maid.

In fiction such situations appear to be easily possible, but in life we cannot count on not being known. Fugitives have often found this out. Sometimes they go to the ends of the earth; but sooner or later, almost surely, someone discovers their identity. Gambling on not being known isn't a very good gamble.

Often people are surprised at meeting friends in far places. But seasoned travelers learn never to be surprised at meeting almost anyone almost anywhere. We may think to lose ourselves in the big city, but, trite as it may seem to say so, it is a small world. And if we engage in unbecoming conduct a thousand miles away, the news will likely get back sooner than we will. Those who let down their standards away from home often learn this and often have cause to be very much embarrassed.

But this isn't the only reason for behaving ourselves well away from home. We ought to have enough common sense and courage and character to do it anyway. Our principles and self-respect should give us reason enough to conduct ourselves in the highest code and character no matter where we are. Personal principles shouldn't shift with geography.

But even if there were no question of principle and no question of conscience, it would still be well to remember that we just can't be sure that we won't be seen by someone whom we shall sometime see again. It isn't ever safe to suppose that the news won't get back. Our record and reputation travel with us. More than that, they often precede us, and show up almost anywhere.

At home or away from home, we cannot rely on not being known. Furthermore, there is no reason why we should—because good conduct and good character are matters of principle, and not merely matters of whether or not we are known. Our identity is indelible—and so is what we are—no matter where we are.

The Making of Memories

Some years ago Gustaf Stromberg, eminent Swedish-American scientist, had some significant things to say in one of his scholarly works concerning the memories of men:

"A study of the nature of memory shows immediately that it must be carried by an immaterial structure. . . . The matter in our brain is continuously changing. . . . And thus we have a 'new' brain after a relatively short time . . . and the necessity of an immaterial living structure in the brain, independent of that of atoms, becomes immediately evident. This structure . . . appears to be indestructible." . . . "We therefore conclude, that there are good reasons for the following important assertion: *The memory of an individual is written in indelible script in space and time.*' " [85]

So much for the assertion of an eminent scientist. This is somewhat reminiscent of the words of William James who said: "Nothing we ever do is in strict scientific literalness wiped out." [86] This in turn is reminiscent of an age-old scriptural truth: "For as he thinketh in his heart, so is he" [87]—and also of the timeless, eternal truth that there is in man something beyond matter; that there is in man an everlasting eternal intelligence.

And now as to the making of memories: We never know when some train of thought will recall something that was long supposed to be forgotten. We may seem to forget the name of the man we met this morning, but from many years back we may remember the most fleeting impression of something relatively unimportant.

There is this to remember about memory: It is easier to make memories than to unmake them. It is easier to remember than to forget. Indeed, it is quite impossible to be sure we have forgotten—anything. And since memory remains, we would do well to look at what we choose to make our memories.

We may think it won't matter to see a sordid scene, to hear a suggestive story, to think an unsavory thought—but this is a shortsighted supposition. The sordid and the unsightly remain in memory as do the inspiring and the beautiful. "As [a man] thinketh in his heart, so is he." And what he thinks and sees and hears, what he chooses to record (insofar as he has any choice), should be such as would be welcome to recall—and not such as he would be ashamed to remember.

"The memory of an individual is written in indelible script in space and time." Surely we shall judge ourselves by the memories we choose to make.

On Coming Too Close...

We remember as youngsters that there was much magic in a magnet—as carefully we would push nails toward it, or other objects of iron, to see at just what point its pull would snap the approaching object to itself. But the moment we discovered that point, it was too late to pull back. We found that we had to stop somewhere short of the magnet's effective field if we didn't want the pull to be completed.

There are other things in life like that. Sometimes we make unsafe assumptions. We might assume that we are strong enough to come close to something and still pull away from it when we want to. We might assume that we are strong enough to swim against the undertow, that we are strong enough to free ourselves from the whirlpool.

Sometimes we seem to be even as the foolish child who pushes his finger toward the whirling fan blade. What makes him do it we do not always know—curiosity? ignorance? sheer foolishness? the spirit of adventure? Call it what we will, the fact remains that if a person proceeds too far in any dangerous direction he is going to find the point at which he is too close.

We might assume that we can sample forbidden

things with safety, that we can expose ourselves to danger and not be in danger, that we can approach unsafe situations and draw away when we want to; but history and experience and a long list of disappointed people have proved that it simply isn't so.

It simply isn't safe to try to find the last point which a person can approach and still save himself. It isn't safe to assume that we can play with an evil without paying a bitter price, or that we can live carelessly without being called to account.

The cliff we don't want to fall over we shouldn't approach the edge of, for we never know when the edge will crumble. We never know when an accident will happen, but we do know that it is less likely to happen if we don't crowd danger too closely, if we "keep out of tight places."

What should be avoided should be altogether avoided. What we don't want to happen, we shouldn't invite to happen. It simply isn't safe to tempt temptation.

A Legacy of Experience

There sometimes seems to be a disposition to assume that the lessons which another generation has learned don't apply to the present. And seemingly on this assumption, young people are often impatient with the counsel and cautioning of parents. But this they should know: that it is more foolish to spurn a legacy of experience than to spurn a legacy of goods or of gold.

There are two ways by which the lessons of life are learned: by our own experience and by the experience of others. When we read, we are drawing upon the experience of others. When we go to school, we are taught the experience of others. We learn of the laws or theories they have discovered, of the conclusions they have come to.

The experience of others is a great heritage, and the more we learn from it the less of life we waste. If every researcher insisted on going back to the beginning to perform all the experiments that all his predecessors had performed, life would largely be wasted in proving what had already been proved. If every explorer were to ignore all previous exploration, life would largely be wasted in finding what had already been found. If travelers were to ignore the road signs and danger signals, life could largely

[171]

be wasted in repeating mistakes that other men have made.

We have a great heritage of revealed and discovered truth. But we lose a lot of life when we ignore what has repeatedly been proved and insist on going back to the beginning again and again.

And as to you who are young and sometimes impatient with the counsel and precautions of parents, this you should know: In their love for you, they are only trying to pass on to you a legacy of experience, even as they would pass on precious heirlooms or a legacy of money or of property. They are only trying to pass on the knowledge of some timeless principles that do not change simply because the times have changed.

The more you can learn from the past, the less you will have to pay for the costly and painful process of trial and error. And deliberately throwing away experience from reliable sources is fully as foolish, if not more foolish, than deliberately throwing away tangibles.

Closing Curtains and Commencements

As each season closes to be followed by each successive season, we become aware that life is a series of scenes separated by closing curtains and commencements. Sometimes these commencements are formally obvious, as on academic occasions, but sometimes we step almost imperceptibly from scene to scene.

The hours move; the days pass; and the years add up, no matter what part we are performing; and the only part we play in time's passing is the purpose to which we put it. We can waste it or use it well. We can fill it full or leave it empty and idle. We can use it for the right things or use it for the wrong things—but we can't "save" time, for it always passes at its own pace.

Sometimes we let the best years for practice and preparation slip by. Perhaps most of us who are older have realized later in life that some things would have been much easier if we had done them when we were younger, for with increasing years and increasing responsibilities more and more we are crowded into living life with less and less time for preparing to live. And it can be difficult and

[173]

discouraging to try to play a part for which we have neglected to prepare.

We say this not so much for us who are older but mostly for you who are younger. We say it because in looking back we can sometimes see how much time we wasted in doing things that didn't mean much, and how much of what we have yet to do could have been done easier earlier. (And in making our choices we must remember all along the way that if we choose to do some things, we choose in effect to pass up other things because here in life as we now know it, time is too short to do everything.)

Time is the very essence of all our opportunities, and we had better do earlier the things that are easier to do earlier, if we would avoid living our lives just a little too late.

* * *

"I remember my youth and the feeling that I could last forever, outlast the sea, the earth, and all men." [88]

—Joseph Conrad

Some Questions of Conscience and Compensation

"... 'tis a blushing, shamefast spirit that mutinies in a man's bosom." [89]

—William Shakespeare

The Question of Compensation

Since Emerson wrote his essay on compensation, it has been difficult to say anything new on the subject. But for a generation that may have forgotten, and for a generation that may not yet have become acquainted with it, perhaps some sentences could well be recalled, among them, these:

"The world looks like . . . a mathematical equation, which, turn it how you will, balances itself." . . .

"A certain compensation balances every gift and every defect." . . . "Things refuse to be mismanaged long." . . . "There is always some leveling circumstance." . . . "You cannot do wrong without suffering wrong." . . . "If you tax too high, the revenue will yield nothing." . . . "In labor as in life there can be no cheating. The thief steals from himself. The swindler swindles himself." . . . "Do the thing, and you shall have the power: but they who do not the thing have not the power." . . . "Men suffer all their life long, under the foolish superstition that they can be cheated. But it is . . . impossible for a man to be cheated by anyone but himself." [90]

So much for Emerson and his essay. But this one thought further we should like to leave: There are some in the world who are willing, some less willing, some unwilling—to work, to serve, to give of themselves. And one of the lessons we earnestly need to remember is that life does not give its choicest blessings and satisfactions to those who deliberately withhold helpfulness and usefulness.

It is true that a willing person sometimes seems to be imposed upon, but for every useful part he performs, he is somehow richly rewarded. Aside from all else, he feels good inside himself; while a niggardly, unwilling nature, which gives only grudgingly, is grudgingly rewarded.

No doubt there will be some cynicism concerning this subject. And it would be difficult to prove to the satisfaction of the cynical just how, precisely, a person would be paid for every service, for every effort, for every activity. We cannot always tell the cynical *precisely* how nature will reward or how the Lord God will return good for good; but as surely as we live, he who withholds his hand from service, he who isn't going to do one stroke more than what he feels is his so-called fair share, is going to miss more than he can calculate. As surely as we live, he who shirks will shrivel inside himself, and he who hides his light loses light. "Every virtue is rewarded, every wrong redressed, in silence and certainty." [90]

The Constancy of Compensation

May we look again at this question of compensation: Sometimes it may seem that rewards are long delayed. Sometimes it may seem that those who are selfish, that those who shirk, that those who engage in sharp practice, that those who follow forbidden ways, acquire an enviable living and live an enviable life. If it seems so, it is because we see only one side—for what is acquired by means that cannot be condoned, is not quite what it sometimes seems to be.

To put it another way: Suppose we assume that the undeserving are sometimes successful. (To assume this would be to assume a narrow definition of success.) But if we knew enough, if we could see all sides (including inside), if we knew all the elements that go into the making of a man, that go into the making of his highest happiness; if we could calculate the full effect of the things that coarsen him, the things that make a callous conscience; the things that refine, that give understanding and appreciation and peace and settled purpose—if we knew all this, we should know that, aside from so-called ultimate reward, there is a constancy of compensation.

There is compensation in the very make-up of a

[179]

man. In the words of William James: "Every smallest stroke of virtue or of vice leaves its never so little scar." [91] Every thought and act and utterance is being counted "among the molecules and nerve cells and fibres." . . . "Nothing we ever do is in strict scientific literalness wiped out." [91] An abused conscience, for example, impairs the capacity for appreciation. "Punishment," added Emerson, "is a fruit that unsuspected, ripens within the flower of the pleasure which concealed it. . . . Seed and fruit cannot be severed; for the effect already blooms in the cause . . . the fruit in the seed." . . . "What will you have? quoth God; pay for it and take it. . . . Thou shalt be paid exactly for what thou hast done, no more, no less." . . . "The cheat, the defaulter, the gambler cannot extort the benefit." . . . "Everything has its price; and if that price is not paid, not that thing but something else is obtained. . . . It is impossible to get anything without its price." [92]

Perpetually and perennially, in ways that we are not always immediately aware of, there is a reward received or a penalty paid for everything we do or fail to do. Aside from ultimate and eternal considerations, there is compensation in the very make-up of man.

Judgment—Every Hour, Every Instant

Sometimes judgment (in the sense of retribution and reward) is thought to be something rather remote—something ultimately to be arrived at but not necessarily now—something such as the "day of judgment" associated with heaven and the hereafter. But judgment doesn't wait (not any more than compensation does) entirely for an eternal future. It is operative in many ways, whether we are aware of it or not. In some measure we judge ourselves every day, every hour, every instant.

"A man cannot speak," said Emerson, "but he judges himself. With his will, or against his will, he draws his portrait to the eye of his companions by every word. Every opinion reacts on him who utters it." [92]

We judge and appraise and classify ourselves constantly by the things we choose to do with our time, our means, our money, by the people and places we prefer, by the selections we make of all of life's activities and offerings. We are, in fact, a living reflection of all that moves in our minds, of every thought and act and utterance—and intent. And what we are essentially, inside ourselves, is in itself a judgment. What we are, judges us as surely as water seeks a common surface.

Some things may seem to go undetected. But none goes unrecorded or unjudged, whether we know it or not. And while we do not know by what process God, our Father, our ultimate Judge, will appraise and reward and punish, we can know that when the picture of our life is rerun, when thoughts and acts and utterances are brought before us, and remembered, we shall sense what we deserve inside ourselves (even as we now do in some degree) and we shall need no outside accuser. We know now when there is a sincere warmth of approval within; we know when there is an inner uneasiness, and when there is cold and comfortless accusation.

We judge ourselves constantly—"in silence and certainty." [92] The only place a man can find real peace is inside himself, and if that is what he wants, he must live to deserve inner peace and approval.

On Outsmarting Other Men

There is another side to this subject of someone
to trust, someone to be safe with, and that is
this: The person who is foolish enough to suppose
that he can outsmart other men, that he can outsmart a law, or a lock, or an audit, or a safety system
is simply outsmarting himself.

It is true that a person might conceal something
for a while. The swindler, the deceiver, the plotter
always has the first advantage because he knows
beforehand what he is plotting. A person, for example, who is planning embezzlement, has some
advantage in timing, because no one else knows
what he has done until after he has done it.

But even though the defrauder, or thief, has a
head start, no one, in any act of life, can, for very
long, count on concealment. And for a man to suppose that he can outsmart other men would seem
to require a peculiar kind of conceit (or stupidity),
for what he says, in substance, is this: that he has
thought of something that others haven't thought
of, or couldn't think of, and he is therefore going
to get away with something. But anyone who is
contemplating some act outside the law, some
fraud, some deception, some evil or unworthy act
had just as well rule out of his calculations the pos-

sibility of secrecy or concealment, because the same kind of mind that can outsmart other men can also catch the kind of mind that can outsmart other men. Thus the cycle completes itself as the outsmarter is outsmarted.

Emerson had some striking things to say on this subject. He used this very phrase: "There is no such thing as concealment. Commit a crime, and the earth is made of glass. Commit a crime, and it seems as if a coat of snow fell on the ground, such as reveals in the woods the track of every partridge and fox and squirrel and mole. You cannot . . . wipe out the foot-track, you cannot draw up the ladder, so as to leave no inlet or clue. Always some damning circumstance transpires." [92]

As young people leave school to enter upon their life's careers and to face their own future, we would burn this into their hearts as one of the greatest lessons of life: play it straight and clean, with honor and honesty, with no deception, no concealment, no taking of anything that isn't yours, no compromising of any principle. Otherwise there is always the long arm of the law—and something longer than the law—something that faces us with the fact of whether or not we are fit to live with ourselves, whether or not we can sleep, whether or not we can feel safe. This kind of peace, this kind of confidence, comes only as it is earned—for a person cannot count on concealment.

A Straight Line...

We recall once more the mathematical maxim that "a straight line is the shortest distance between two points." In a day when so many people find themselves paying a price for forgetting it, this rule of life would well be unforgettably remembered.

In the first place, in forgetting it, there follows the factor of inefficiency—for a person who departs from a straight course almost inevitably carries on a conversation with his conscience. And a person who is carrying on a conversation with his conscience can't be very efficient. It is difficult to do two things at once, for any of us. And if we have our minds on things we shouldn't have done, we aren't so effectively thinking of the things we should be doing. Uneasiness within always adversely affects efficiency.

Then there is also the question of the ability to turn back. There is a time, to begin with, in the decisions of all of us, when right or wrong is only a matter of one step—a step straight forward, or a side step. But the farther we go on any wrong road, the more time we lose, and the more costly it is to turn back. It was Montaigne who remarked that "the births of all things are weak and tender,

[185]

and therefore we should have our eyes intent on beginnings." [93]

The beginnings of habits are small and weak. The beginnings of falsehoods are small and weak. The "little" compromises of honesty, the "little" forms of cheating, the small infractions of law, the unauthorized "borrowing" (so-called) of something that isn't ours, the inconspicuous little lie—all such beginnings, all such departures from a straight line, may seem insignificant at first, but, if unchecked, they move to the point where turning back is difficult and costly (but not nearly so costly as not turning back!).

Happiness is the aim and object of all of us, and there simply isn't any sincere and satisfying happiness to be found, there isn't any way to peace of mind, except to move straightforwardly forward, with truth and integrity, and with no apology to make to any man, or to the Father of us all, or to us, inside ourselves. In matters of character and conduct, as well as in mathematics, a straight line is the shortest short cut—the shortest distance between two points.

"Telling" the Truth

There is a sentence from one of the writings of Samuel Taylor Coleridge that suggests a deeply significant subject: "Veracity," he said, "does not consist in saying, but in the intention of communicating truth." [94]

Too often it is assumed that the truth has been told if someone simply says the right words. Too often it is assumed that a person has told the truth when actually he has told a half-truth and withheld the other half. But no one has told the truth when he has deliberately left a false impression, no matter what words he has used or how he has used them.

Men might mislead other men by the inflection of their voices, by insinuation and innuendo, by gesture, by what they suggest rather than by what they say, and by what they leave unsaid. They might say so much and imply much more, and then hide behind the literal limits of language. In many such ways men frequently falsify, and often we could not legally prove that they had perpetrated an untruth, yet morally we may know that they intended not to tell the truth.

There are those who, as Isaiah indicts them, "make a man an offender for a word," [95] those who resort to slick, legal loopholes, those who insincerely

rely upon the letter of the law and ignore every intention of honor and honesty. Whatever our words we shall ultimately have to answer for the broad intent of our actions and utterances—and not merely for legal terminology or technicalities, not merely for the letter of the law.

The whole intent of a man, what he means to do and what he means not to do, what he means to say and what he means not to say, what he thinks in his heart, what he is in his soul, are all involved in "telling" the truth, for which we are all accountable before our fellow men and before our eternal Father.

God grant that in our time we may hear and know and speak and write and live the truth, and not rely on tricky technicalities or legal loopholes or ambiguous utterance that is a mere mask for falsehood. "Veracity does not consist in saying, but in the intention of communicating truth." The mere appearance of truthfulness is not enough.

A Matter of Semantics...

Perhaps it has always been so; certainly during our day it seems increasingly to have been so: that custom and connotation have changed the meaning of words, and that men have found new ways for uttering old ideas.

Diseases that once were called by common names are likely at any time to take on the technical terminology of medical men. And certainly the words that describe the philosophies and political persuasions of people have been made over and modified. Democracy, freedom, liberal, reactionary, and many other terms have at times been appropriated and misappropriated for some peculiar purposes.

Another field that has been affected are the words concerning guilt and blame and sin. Indeed it sometimes seems that there are those who would altogether remove from men any sense of responsibility for their own thoughts and acts and utterances. But there are still laws and principles, commandments and causes that lead to consequences, no matter what we may have come to call our acts and utterances.

This is the law of life. Constantly as well as ultimately we pay a price for errors and indiscretions—

notwithstanding any disposition to call sin something else—notwithstanding new terms, new colorings, new connotations that sometimes make things sound as if they were something other than what they are. We can call a disease by another name, but it still manifests the same symptoms. We can call an evil by another name, but it still manifests the same results.

If we need a more acute terminology, if we need to sharpen our semantics, certainly we should do so. We should feel free to add names and words and technical terms as occasion may require. But heaven keep us from the fallacy of supposing that we have changed the nature of the thing by calling it another name. Heaven keep us from supposing that we absolve ourselves, or are in any way relieved of the law of cause and effect, by turning to technical terms. It simply isn't so.

The Sound Is Silenced...

Sometimes there are sounds which at first we are only vaguely aware of, intrusive, insistent sounds that are all around us, but which don't quite break through to our full consciousness, sounds which are somehow partly shut out from our senses: the throbbing of a motor, the roar of traffic, the worrisome sound of the wind, the hiss of escaping steam, the pervasive sound of an air-conditioning system, the droning of a fan.

Often we are aware of such sounds as an unpleasant obligato—as something that makes us tense and ill at ease. And then suddenly something is shut off; suddenly the sound ceases—and there is quiet, blessed quiet; and a sense of relief and peace. And only then do we become altogether aware of the disturbing effects of the sound we partly sensed, as we feel the relief and relaxing that come when it suddenly ceases.

There is a striking parallel in this physical phenomenon with the insistent unheard sounds that sometimes make us inwardly ill at ease: the obligato of an unquiet conscience; of jealousies and jarring thoughts; of inner resistance and resentments; the accusations that follow our failing to do what we know we should do, our failing to perform as fully as we should perform; the accusations that come when we have turned away someone we could have helped; the futility that follows too much striving for things that don't matter too much—for false pride and empty position; the discontent of wasting time; the inner accusations that come with unkindness, with hate and harsh words; with judging others unjustly.

And then there comes (or can come) a release, a peace, as if an offending sound were silenced— the peace that follows the changing of an inner attitude, the admitting of an error, the leaving of bad habits behind, of putting aside false pride, of moving to make wrongs right, of ceasing to do what was not right.

There comes (or can come) a blessed silencing of the inner jarring sounds. There come (or can come with apology, with prayer, with sincere repentance) such peace and blessed relief as come when a disquieting sound ceases within our very souls.

* * *

"I feel within me
A peace above all earthly dignities
A still and quiet conscience." [96]
—Shakespeare and Fletcher

Of Peace and Repentance

"He that repents is angry with himself;
I need not be angry with him." [97]
—Benjamin Whichcote

Why Leave It So Late?

On a certain journey not long ago some travelers encountered one of those untamed onslaughts of the elements which man, despite all his previous preparations, is never quite prepared for. It became a question of survival, or of fear lest they should not survive. And afterward, one who was there soberly said: "There were some people who talked to the Lord that night, who had not talked to him for a long time."

It is true that times of emergency, of danger, of fear, of stress, of urgent need often bring us to an earnest awareness of our dependence upon Providence. And when, in extreme circumstances, we are pressed to petition Him to whom we haven't talked for a long time, the question may well be asked: "Why leave it so late?"

We never know, not any of us, when we are going to need help or when we shall wish we had done some things we didn't do. We never know how our business ventures are going. We often assume that profits or success are certain when some unforeseen circumstance enters in, and we find that they weren't so certain.

Sometimes in newly acquired affluence, shortsighted people assume that they won't need their old friends—or that they won't need anyone. But fortunes change; reverses come; and we often find that we desperately need those from whom we have severed ourselves.

There is no one so big, no one so secure, no one who can so far foresee the future, but what he needs to keep his house and his life in order, his record straight, and his friendships in repair. A man who needs friends had better have them before he needs them. There is no one so wise or so self-sufficient but what he needs the services of others. And when the storm has broken, when the accident has happened, when the need is upon us, it may be a little too late. It is always too late to take out insurance to cover a previous casualty.

Of course we can repent. But even *that* we should not leave too late. We are dependent upon others always; we are dependent upon Providence always; and we ought to be on good terms with our family and friends, with ourselves, with life, and with our Father in heaven all the time. Humility and gratitude and consideration for all others and a prayerful approach to every problem is the safest insurance against all eventualities. And a good question to ask ourselves in all the ways of life is, "Why leave it so late?"

On Multiplying Mistakes

Perhaps we have all had the experience of trying to find a place we haven't been before, and of turning off the right road—and then somehow sensing that we *had* turned off the right road. But despite the warning sense within us, we may doggedly have pursued the wrong road until we arrived at a dead end, or until we had gone so far that we had lost much time and had much distance to retrace.

There are many ways in which men find themselves on wrong roads, and seemingly there are many reasons why they don't sooner turn back to the right one: sometimes because of stubbornness, of pride or perverseness; sometimes because of the fallacy of supposing that if a person has taken one wrong step he had just as well take two; that if he has slipped somewhat he had just as well slip farther; that if he has made one mistake, it doesn't matter too much if he makes more. These are all flagrant fallacies that cause carelessness to lead to more carelessness, misconduct to more misconduct, to the ultimate hardening of habits, and to heartbreak and unhappiness.

It was said of the prodigal son that he "came to himself." [98] But it was only after he had gone a long way in the wrong direction and after he had lost his inheritance and his self-respect.

If those who have erred would come to themselves sooner, they wouldn't have so far to return. There is no reason why a man who has made a mistake should multiply his mistakes. The sooner a wrong course is corrected, the less the time lost, and the less the penalty imposed, and the sooner is found the peace that comes with the consciousness of being on the right road.

Let no foolish pride, no stubborn perverseness cause delay in correcting a wrong course. To recall the words of William James: Men "can alter their lives by altering their attitudes. . . ." [99] Let false pride be pushed aside; let men come to themselves sooner, let the blessed principle of repentance enter the picture; wherever they are—for the awareness of moving in the right direction, after having moved in a wrong one, is a wonderful awareness.

The Price of Repenting

Repentance doesn't appear to be very popular. Prophets have been made martyrs for proclaiming it; nations and peoples have died rather than do anything about it. But however unpopular or unpalatable, repentance is one of the greatest, most satisfying principles that God has given—for we are none of us perfect; we, none of us, turn in a perfect performance; we are, none of us, without earnest urgent need of the principle of repentance, and without it our lives would be futile and frustrated.

In a sense, any improvement is repentance—any straightening of a road, any saving of danger or distance; any improving of a process, any abandoning of old errors or of inefficient ways is repentance. Repentance is a basic principle of progress.

Now as to some, among many things to repent of: We could well consider repentance from procrastination, from wasting time, from withholding willing work; repentance for incurring debts too willingly that we have little prospect of repaying; repentance for too little appreciation of our loved ones, or for what is done for us by others; repentance from letting life slip by without giving our attention to things that matter most, or for not keeping closer in counsel and companionship to those who mean the most; repentance from indifference to what we ought to be doing; repentance from brooding too much upon the past; and for too little faith in the future.

Now as to the nature of repentance: It is more than saying we're sorry, more than embarrassment, more than the discomfort of being caught, more than fear, more than an effort to avoid punishment or penalties. It is a sincere change within, a sincere turning away, as suggested by the Saviour when he said: "Go, and sin no more." [100] Such repentance lets us live with ourselves with quiet conscience and leads to peace and progress.

People have sometimes supposed that repentance was too high priced. They have looked at what they would have to give up, at appetites they would have to curb, at habits they would have to break or abandon, at things they would have to set aside, and have forgotten the fact that no matter what the price of repenting, it is never so high as the price of not repenting—and no later hour is ever better for the purpose of repenting than this very hour is.

To Begin Again

Sometimes we hear someone say, "I wish I could begin again; I wish I could live life over with what I know now." It is not an uncommon wish, but time cannot be turned back, and in life no road can be retraveled just as once it was.

We can't begin back where we were. But we can begin where we are, and in an eternity of existence, this is a reassuring fact. There is virtually nothing that a man cannot turn away from if he really wants to. There is virtually nothing that he cannot improve. There is virtually no habit that he cannot give up if he will sincerely set his will to do so and will sincerely seek and accept help—the help of others and the help of his Father in heaven.

But our interest in being better, in improving upon the past, in turning to new ways, in leaving habits behind, sometimes seems to be a wish without a will, a wish with resignation, a wish that assumes that about all we can do is wish that we could go back. But there is no one who cannot be better by turning toward the ways in which he should walk, however far he may have walked the wrong way.

Without the principle and possibility of repentance there would be little incentive left for any of us—for all of us need it, whether we know it or not. And though we cannot go back and begin where we were, we can begin where we are, wherever we are. No one is justified in assuming that a habit that has hold of him is unbreakable or that a poor past performance cannot be improved.

The wish to begin again, the wish to live life over with what we know now, is a wish that cannot be realized. There is no turning back to any point or period of the past. But if we can't begin where we *were*, we *can* begin where we *are*, and the memory of a wrong road is blessedly dimmed by the reality of being on the right road.

"What's Past Is Prologue"

There is a comforting line from Shakespeare which in one short sentence has much to suggest: "What's past is prologue." [101] It is a plea for hope, for new beginnings, for not brooding about what cannot now be reclaimed or recalled, a plea for faith in the future—a plea for repentance. No matter what we have done or failed to do, our opportunity is from here on. And blessedly, through the principle of repentance, "What's past *is* prologue."

Over and over we are comforted by this strengthening, sustaining thought: Our Father in heaven knows us. He knows our hearts; He knows our difficulties and desires; He knows our mistakes, our problems, our sorrows, our shortcomings. He knows the motives by which we are moved and the influences by which we are swayed. He knows why we do what we do and why we fail to do what we should have done. He knows the reasons we fall short of being the best we might be.

He knows our needs and he has sent us here not to fail but to succeed. And if we will only give Him an opportunity in our lives, He will help to lift us to our highest possibilities and happiness and peace and progress. And whatever we have done or fallen short of doing, "What's past is prologue," and before us, with His help, is the opportunity to improve our performance.

If we will prayerfully approach Him and invite Him into our daily acts and utterances, we shall find the sunlight dispelling the shadows.

There is no more helpful principle in life than the principle of sincere repentance. And whatever we may have failed in as a people, as a nation, as mothers, fathers, friends, as children, as loved ones, as citizens in a troubled society, the hope we have is in the great power and privilege of repentance. "What's past is prologue"—and the everlasting future is before us to improve.

* * *

"With the morning cool repentance came." [102]

—Walter Scott

On Surviving Sorrows

"It is wrong to sorrow without ceasing." [103]

—Homer

On a Dark and Sleepless Night...

A sentence recently read offers these words of wise and comforting counsel: "Do not distress yourself with dark imaginings. Many fears are born of fatigue and loneliness." [104] No doubt most of us at times have turned our troubles over in the hours of the night, when sleep has fled from us. And in the dark hours of night troubles tend to be multiplied and magnified.

If our loved ones are out and overdue, it isn't difficult to imagine dark and dire things—in the hours of the night. And then, finally, as they return, well and whole, the load is lifted, and likely we wonder that we so much feared and fretted.

The shades of discouragement and despondency are darker and deeper in the hours of night, and small things loom large, and large things sometimes seem utterly insurmountable. In the restless hours of night it isn't difficult to imagine all manner of maladies and malignancies. Indeed, on a dark and leepless night, with all its tossings and turnings, we could churn up many troubles inside our-selves.

Job poignantly complained that "wearisome

nights are appointed to me. When I lie down, I say, When shall I arise, and the night be gone? and I am full of tossings to and fro unto the dawning of the day." [105]

But despite all real or imagined difficulty and discouragement that come with darkness, the dawn does come, and the load does lighten with the coming of daylight. Even when our worries are real, and even when they don't altogether disappear, the light of day tends to lift and lighten them.

Thank God for light, for the dawning of each new day, for the reassuring brightness of the sun —for much of what darkens and disturbs us doesn't seem so darkly serious, so utterly insurmountable, in the daylight as it did at night. And because the darkness distorts, because it clouds and conceals, in darkness we should make no needless decisions and reach no needless conclusions, but wait to look at our problems in the light—wait for the natural waking hour, when "the morning breaks; the shadows flee." [106]

Harboring Our Hurts

No doubt the course of history has many times been altered because someone has had his feelings hurt. There are some classic examples that suggest themselves, one such at the siege of Troy with Achilles sulking in his tent. But for every such that has been publicly cited, there are millions more where the lives of people have been blighted, some seriously and some superficially, because someone has had hurt feelings.

Sometimes the consequences of hurt feelings, of personal offense, have been appallingly serious, far out of proportion to the first cause, as men have stubbornly misunderstood one another and families and others implacably have fought and feuded (like Shakespeare's Capulets and Montagues) and the lives of the innocent have been blighted (like Romeo and Juliet), and irreparable damage has been done—because someone has had his pride injured, because someone has had his feelings hurt.

It is true that people are often thoughtless; often inconsiderate, blunt, undiplomatic, sometimes cruel; and often deal with others the wrong way. But men being as they are, imperfect as they are, so long as we move among them, we are sometimes going to have our feelings hurt, even when others don't know they have hurt us. There likely isn't one of us who hasn't been hurt (and likely there isn't one of us who hasn't hurt others).

But if too easily we assume a martyr's role, if we nurture and magnify our hurts, if we withdraw ourselves from fellowship, from activity, and brood and let our injuries fester, and sulk too long in our tents, we do serious damage to ourselves, our families, our friends, and to the causes we might have served.

As in the healing process following some kinds of surgery, so hurts of the heart, hurt pride and injured feelings can sooner be healed if we don't nurse them too long, if we are sooner up, and out, and active.

Life goes on whether we go with it or not, and sitting aside in hurt silence when there are things to be done is one unfortunate way of letting life waste away. We do ourselves great damage by languishing too long in injured inactivity.

We commend to all these words of an unidentified author: "In the very depths of your soul, dig a grave; let it be as some forgotten spot to which no path leads; and there in the eternal silence bury the wrongs which you have suffered. Your heart will feel as if a load had fallen from it, and a divine peace come to abide with you." [107]

Hidden in Their Hearts

Most of the men and women who move about us from day to day are carrying their share of trouble and disappointment and sorrow hidden within their hearts; and we, with unseeing eyes, often walk roughshod over them, not knowing their cares, not understanding their burdens. So often we misjudge those whose situation and circumstances we do not know.

Those whom we meet in an impersonal way in the places we patronize and those whom we pass in all the crowded ways and walks of life may seem at times to be distant, to be sullen, preoccupied, impolite or inattentive to our wants and wishes. And we, with our absence of understanding, often ignore their heavy hearts, their troubled thoughts, their sorrows, their pressing problems, and the weight of their worries.

Every man's burdens are important to him. Every man's worries affect his attitude and his work. No man is a mere machine. And yet sometimes it seems that we expect the same kind of mechanical constancy from a man that we do from a machine.

If we want the answer to why people are as they are and why they do what they sometimes do, we shall need to know more about what is weighing on their thoughts or what is hidden in their hearts. A quarrel, an illness at home, worry about a wayward youngster, a personal disappointment, apprehension about an ailment, anxiety about money matters, friction, frustration—all can and do alter the attitudes and efficiency and outlook and actions of all of us.

And if the men we meet, the people we patronize, those who serve us and those with whom we associate, and those whom we casually see in public and other places—if they aren't always as it seems to us they should be, there may be some real reason that we would readily understand if we only knew enough. At least it would be well to withhold judgment and to apply patience and to refrain from unkind comment and hasty conclusions where we are not sufficiently informed—where we are somewhat short of understanding as to the thoughts and hearts and feelings of our fellows. God grant us the wisdom to withhold judgment when we don't know enough.

* * *

"Every man has his secret sorrows which the world knows not; and oftentimes we call a man cold when he is only sad." [108]
—Henry W. Longfellow

Surviving the First Shock...

In any loss or injury or illness or accident, the first sharpness of pain, the first fear, the first disappointment, the first sense of sorrow, may seem almost unbearable. But mercifully, in the case of physical injury, usually the first sharpness subsides —enough at least to be bearable. And mercifully, this is true to some extent in other things also. Time—even a little time—tends to dull the edge of anguish, and the things we thought we couldn't learn to live with (or learn to live without) when we have to, we do somehow learn to live with (or without).

Seneca had something to say on this subject some twenty centuries ago: "No one could endure adversity," he said, "if while it continued, it kept the same violence that its first blows had. . . . No state is so bitter that a calm mind cannot find in it some consolation. . . . It is possible to soften what is hard, to widen what is narrow, and burdens will press less heavily upon those who bear them skillfully." [109]

The shock, the fear, the first sharp pain, the sudden sorrow, do soften somewhat as time takes over. And in any case, we can't afford to assume that anything which, for the moment, is unalterable, is unbearable. We all have to learn to live with some unwanted circumstances and situations—but blessedly, with faith and work and patient, purposeful waiting, the first acuteness does subside, and we learn to adjust our lives to our losses, to our disappointments, to our failures and frustrations.

To repeat the sentence from Seneca: "No one could endure adversity if while it continued, it kept the same violence that its first blows had." And we may well be grateful for faith in an everlasting plan and purpose, for faith in compensation and in an ultimate, just judgment—and for time that dulls the edge of shocks and sorrows, even when it doesn't undo them.

If Ye Have Found Faith

What is this faith that is so freely referred to? . . . faith in God, faith as an antidote to fear, faith for a future that cannot be foreseen, faith as a sustaining force in misfortune and sorrow and uncertainty, faith in eternal plan and purpose and in limitless personal progress and everlasting reunion with those we love, faith in "the substance . . . of things not seen."[110] It is not as the certain knowledge of things that we can physically feel and see and taste and touch. If it were, it would not be faith. It is trust, belief, conviction; an inner sense and assurance—a principle and power which prevents the uncertainty of the future from destroying the peace and purpose of the present; which brings comfort in sorrow, and sweet sleep in uncertainty.

We read that faith "is the gift of God." [111] But if a man feels that he hasn't the gift of faith, must he merely sit by and envy those who have, and endure the sense of loss and loneliness and the susceptibility to cynicism and the feeling of frustration that are so frequently the lot of those who live without faith?

Fortunately, the prospect is not so unpromising— not even for those who feel that they haven't faith, not even for those who are skeptical and discouraged, for in all of us there is a live spark of faith that may only require kindling, no matter how faint it sometimes seems.

Anciently these words were uttered to some who were searching for faith: "But behold, if ye will awake and arouse your faculties . . . and exercise a particle of faith, yea, even if ye can no more than desire to believe, let this desire work in you. . . . Then . . . ye shall reap the rewards of your faith." [112]

The sentence suggests restatement: Even if you can do no more than desire to believe, let this desire work within until there is an awareness within of a growing gift of faith that gives strength and comfort and peace and sweet assurance—"sweet above all that is sweet . . . and ye shall feast upon this fruit even until ye are filled." [112] Blessed are ye if ye have found faith.

Facing Life on Our Feet

From all observable evidence, it would appear that man was made for movement—that he was made to face life on his feet, moving, working, thinking, growing, solving his problems, and meeting his obligations with freedom and faith. Life itself means moving. Nothing stands still, and there is nothing in nature or in holy writ that does not suggest that man was made to face each day with work and faith. Indeed, in the account of the Creation, the Lord God said that man should have dominion over all the earth and told him to replenish and subdue it.

These are words of much meaning. They impose upon us all the obligation to act on our environment, and they give us little justification for succumbing easily to circumstances and situations. And we should also act upon ourselves, and not be content to be always as we are. Knowledge can be increased. Abilities can be improved upon. Appetites can be overcome. Desires can be subdued. Weaknesses can be conquered. Life is a process of eternal progression, and all of us are expected to play our part in the eternal performance.

Even the impaired are expected to perform what part they can perform. If we can't move out on our feet, we can move to whatever degree we can move. And when we can't move, we can think.

The promise of dominion that man was given over all the earth implies also control over ourselves. In the words of Leonardo da Vinci: "You will never have a greater or lesser dominion than that over yourself." [113] Life was meant to be faced on our feet, with freedom and faith; and it was not meant that we should succumb to circumstances and situations—nor to ourselves—but that we should ever improve upon our own past, on the road of eternal progress. "You will never have a greater or lesser dominion than that over yourself."

"And Thou Shalt Be Built up..."

There comes to mind a phrase remembered from a childhood game of forfeits: "Heavy, heavy hangs over thy poor head." If we were to emphasize the negative side of the passing scenes, all of us could live fearful, trembling lives. Momentous forces and issues of ominous import do hang heavily over our heads—and rumors and reports of adverse events could well remind us of these words of the Master as recorded by Matthew:

"And ye shall hear of wars and rumors of wars. . . . For nation shall rise against nation, and kingdom against kingdom: and there shall be famines, and pestilences, and earthquakes, in divers places. . . . And then shall many be offended, and shall betray one another, and shall hate one another." [114] So reads the scriptural record. But it also says that "he that shall endure unto the end, the same shall be saved." [114]

Difficult problems aren't peculiar to our time. Men have lived through difficulties and discouragement in other days. And this is not a time for the trembling, timid living of life—but for pursuing it from day to day with work, faith, repentance, patience and prayerful purpose.

No matter what hangs over our heads, life goes on, and we go with it—and children must have their chance, their happiness, their education, their opportunities. Youth must have faith and work and purpose and preparation for the future—for there will always be a future, and we can meet it knowing that men have met it before.

The Lord God is still alive, and, as we are willing to keep close to Him, will not leave us alone. Furthermore, there is the assurance of eternal continuance. The human spirit, the human soul, all and each of us as ourselves, will always survive. And while we cannot be indifferent to what hangs over our heads, yet peace and quiet and satisfying purpose can and do come even in unsettled scenes.

"Acquaint . . . thyself with him," counsels an Old Testament text, "and be at peace: . . . make thy prayer unto him, and he shall hear thee, . . . and thou shalt be built up." [115]

And finally, above the clamor and confusion, come the questions and the answering assurance spoken by our Saviour: "Why are ye so fearful? how is it that ye have no faith? . . . And he arose, and rebuked the wind, and said unto the sea, Peace, be still. And the wind ceased, and there was a great calm." [116]

* * *

"Sorrow is a disease in which every patient must treat himself." [117]

—Voltaire

The Unanswered Questions

"I hear the message well enough; what I lack is faith." [118]

—Goethe

The Unanswered Questions...

No doubt all of us are troubled at times by the unanswered questions of life. No doubt all of us are given to wondering at times about the point and purpose of many things, and even to wondering why we are here. Such thoughts may sometimes come because we are too close to the commonplace activities of each day—too close really to see ourselves or to see the over-all objectives.

If we could just step aside from the rush and routine to which too many of us are too much tied, we could get a fresher perspective and picture and could come closer to answering the question that men for ages have asked: "Why *are* we here?"

Life is short and swiftly moving for all of us, no matter how long we live. And if there were no more purpose in it than is sometimes superficially seen, we should have cause for frustration and for some cynicism. But as a counter-remedy to these recurring feelings of frustration, let each man ask of himself as if he had never heard it questioned or considered: "Why *are* we here on earth?"

While we do not understand all of life's promise and possibilities, we may take unto our hearts the certainty and assurance that we are here as part of a glorious, eternal plan and purpose. We are here because a loving Father gave us the gift of life, gave us a period of preparation for eternal opportunities. We are here to develop faith, to seek knowledge, to think with freedom, to exercise our individual agency, to seek and to accept truth. We are not here primarily for pleasure, although happiness is an important part of the plan. We are not here primarily for the wealth of this world, although the good things of the earth may rightfully be ours—as we work for them.

We are here to learn and not willfully to remain in ignorance, to keep the commandments, to conquer ourselves, to learn to live together. And when we fumble and fall short, which all of us do, there is always the comforting, sustaining thought that we were sent here by a loving Father, who sent us not to fail but to succeed. He understands our hearts, our problems, our difficulties. He understands us and our needs. He expects of us a good and honest and sincere performance. He does not expect of us a presently impossible perfection—but with our willingness, He will help us to return to Him with the purpose of this life completed, and with glorious, everlasting opportunities before us, with those we love. And despite recurring discouragement and sometimes weariness along the way, the hope, the promise, the certainty of things to come makes all the effort infinitely worth while.

On Beginning to Believe...

We hear much concerning the subject of faith: that it will move mountains,[119] that it is the "evidence of things not seen," [120] that with it all things are possible. And altogether all we learn of it leads us to know that faith is indeed a great and desirable gift.

But suppose a man doesn't have faith. Suppose he wants to believe, but doesn't know how to go about beginning to believe. We must frankly face the fact that it seems easier for some men to believe than it does for others. And so comes the question: How does a person go about to begin to believe?

First of all, it would seem that he must want to. It is hard for an utterly unwilling person to begin to believe. But every man lives more by faith than is sometimes supposed. Every person who looks ahead at life, who makes any plan for the future, is doing so partly on faith, for no man knows how much future there is for him within the limits of this life.

Every man who steps into any kind of conveyance is, in a sense, declaring his faith, for he thereby commits himself to some uncertain circumstances. In a similar sense, every person who takes a prescription or submits himself to surgery shows some faith. Any person who eats food which he himself has not processed or prepared is proceeding in part on faith.

Every man who makes an investment has faith. Every man who travels to a country he hasn't seen has faith—faith that he will find it. Everyone who counts on anything beyond this very instant, has a kind of faith within him.

Of course, this isn't the kind of faith implied in some discussions of the subject; but neither, in fact, is it so far from it—*for if a man can believe in some things unseen, he ought also to be able to believe in other things unseen.*

We have to trust the Lord God for so many things—for life, for food, for rainfall, for the succession of the seasons, for all that pertains to tomorrow. For everything that isn't past or present we have to have faith. So every man has much more faith than is sometimes supposed and can have yet much more, for "faith is not to have a perfect knowledge." [121] But it comes or increases with wanting to, with working for, with a willingness to begin to believe, to keep the commandments, to test the promises, to prove the principles, to proceed with faithful performance, for "by faithfulness faith is earned." [122] As summarized in a sentence from the Saviour: "If any man will do his will, he shall know of the doctrine." [123]

The Faith within Us...

May we look further for a moment at a conclusion already arrived at: that every man
has more faith within himself than he sometimes
supposes—not only faith in tangible and touchable
factors and forces, but faith also in the unseen,
untouchable intangibles, and in the eternal future.
It was meant that men should live in part by faith;
and even the cynic has more faith than he himself
sometimes supposes.

One evidence of our faith is that all of us do
some planning for the future. We do not, not any
of us, do all our living altogether in the present or
the past; and any thought for the future carries
with it an element of faith.

Another evidence is the inherent awareness within us of our own enduring identity, of the perpetua-
tion of personality by which we are and always
shall be distinguishable from all others. The evidence is within and all around us: We cannot
imagine ourselves as being nothing. We cannot
imagine ourselves as being anything except ourselves. All the yearnings we have, all the awareness
within, all the reason, law and order—our intelligence, talents, personality, character and all the
intimations of immortality within us—all give evi-

dence, assurance, certainty, of the eternal plan and purpose of Him who made us in His image.

This faith inborn within us was placed there for a purpose: to help to give us an awareness of whence we came, and why we're here, and what we can become. And all the unessential things with which we sometimes so much load our lives, the fineries and fashions, the elaborate equipment of comfort and convenience, the many things which most men have never known, could all be missing, and still life would be meaningful beyond measure because the things that matter most, our lives, our loved ones, continue always and forever.

It is this faith which is in fact "the substance of things hoped for, the evidence of things not seen"; [124] it is this faith that sustains us in our failures and frustrations, in discouragement, in sorrow and sickness; it is this faith that assures us of the love and wisdom and fairness and justice of a loving Father, whose purpose is to bring to pass our happiness and peace and everlasting progress. It is this faith that gives us patience to wait for the ultimate, unseen answers. Thank God for faith which grows to greater faith, for faith by which men can and do endure in faithfulness and faith.

When a Mouse Falls into a Meal Sack . . .

There is an old Dutch proverb that reads, "When a mouse falls into a meal sack, he thinks he is the miller himself" [125]—which suggests something of the sincere humility that all of us should feel in great degree.

We admire great art and the artist—but the painting at best only simulates something seen in the handiwork of God. It may be so well done that it *seems* to have the breath of life, but it doesn't *have* the breath of life. Statuary in clay, in stone, in bronze, delineating beauty of form and face, of muscle and movement, is a thing of beauty only because it simulates and suggests something seen in the work of Him who created us all. At its most beautiful best it lacks the very breath of life.

Let's look a moment in another direction: We are deeply grateful for the discoveries men have made in medicine: for so-called miracle drugs, for skillful diagnosis, and for delicate surgery, but the most skilled of men can only aid the physical functions. He can't create them. He can assist nature, but he can't determine the ultimate outcome. He and all of us must watch and wait when the issues of life and death are in the balance.

The scientist in every field discovers a few laws and uses them to remarkable and miraculous ends, but he doesn't make the laws; he doesn't create the processes; he doesn't make a lifeless thing a living thing. He uses; he observes; he waits; and he wonders.

Sometimes we think great thoughts, new and thrilling and wonderful to us, and then later we find that they have been thought and recorded by many minds, many times, in many places—thoughts that suggest a surpassing Source of truth and of inspiration, of laws and of learning—and failure to recognize the source of all such is an unhappy error.

Because we paint a picture, because we mold a metal, because we carve stone, because we "make" and administer a medicine, because we learn laws, because we can in a measure change the form of things and control some physical functions, does not mean that we are the makers of the things we use or of the laws we learn or of the life we live. And as we see so much of what is made, and lest we think too little of the Maker, we may well remember a homely and humbling proverb: "When a mouse falls into a meal sack, he thinks he is the miller himself."

The Light That Leads to Further Light

Men seem to have an urgent sense of searching for something that they are not now aware of having seen. They are not content with only what their hands can touch, with only what is immediately evident and obvious. And in this searching there sometimes comes a sense of thinking something seemingly for the first time—and yet somehow seeming to remember the same thought from far back—from some distant scene, from some far-forgotten place. And sometimes things are heard which the mortal ear cannot recall having heard before, but which somehow strike a certain inner sense of truth, a deeply satisfying conviction within the very soul. Nor does it seem to be unusual to experience that which seems new and yet which somehow seems not to be new.

Such thoughts suggest inherently within each man an immortal, eternal intelligence—and such thoughts bring to mind these lines from Wordsworth:

> Our birth is but a sleep and a forgetting;
> The soul that rises with us, our life's star,
> Hath had elsewhere its setting,
> And cometh from afar . . .[126]

All through the centuries men have searched because of some inner sense, some light within that led them on to further light, some faith within that told them that there was yet to be found that which they had not yet found. Indeed, most of the significant discoveries that men have made come because of an inner faith in something unseen—an awareness within that moves us on beyond ourselves. And with this inner urging there comes a kind of wholesome discontent, a restless reaching from something that once was to something greater that will yet be.

And so man moves on the eternal path of progress, led if he will by the light which lighteth every man—a light which shows the petty things of life for what they are, which makes the difficulties, the discouragements, the disappointments endurable; which gives patience for the unsolved problems and the unanswered questions, and gives faith for the search and assurance for the future.

Faith, Work, Patience

The New Year does not last long. And despite its festivities, it is somewhat sobering—sobering for many reasons, and in part because of some uncertainties. But sometimes we overemphasize uncertainty. We live with it always and everywhere, and if we were too constantly concerned with the uncertainty of passing and impermanent things, our lives would be forever fearful—for all that lies beyond this very instant is in a sense uncertain. And we should have the faith to plan solidly for the future and not overemphasize uncertainty.

Faith is indispensable in any formula for a New Year. Other indispensable elements to be added are work and patience—a full measure of each. We must be willing to work without knowing all the outcome in advance. And as to patience, we must be willing to wait for final answers (not to cease the search—but not to force or fabricate the answers where they are not in evidence).

So far as this present time is concerned, "Life is a tent for a night," [127]—Emerson observed, but beyond is the infinite and eternal, and as we live according to the best knowledge we have, "doing broad justice where we are, by whomsoever we deal with" [127] in the circumstances in which we find ourselves, and shun false pride and pettiness, the Lord God will see that fairness and justice and equitable opportunity come to each of us; and He will not leave us alone nor let anything be lost, nor any good go unrewarded.

Thank God that there are values that endure always and forever. Thank God for truth, for freedom to search for it, for freedom to accept it; for faith in the eternal future; for patience to wait for the missing pieces to be put in place; for patience to reserve judgment while men argue with one another of things they do not know; for patience to wait for the clouds of speculation to be cleared, for theories to be proved or unproved; patience to wait for the final answers.

God grant us faith, work, patience and a little time to live the goodness of life with our loved ones, to live above the contentious controversies, and to see the eternal certainties beyond the uncertainties, and to walk in prayerful humility with Him who gave us everlasting life and who keeps Creation in its course.

* * *

"Lord, I believe; help thou mine unbelief." [128]

—Spoken to Jesus by the father of
a stricken child

The Question of Everlasting Life

". . . but some doubted." [129]
—Matthew

Whence and Why and Whither?

Not long ago I watched a loving family before an open grave, as the casket of a beloved silver-haired father was lowered to its resting place. There was calm. There was peace, and no evidence of irreconcilable sorrow. In their hearts there seemed to be assurance that all that is most loved in life is everlasting.

And then I thought of other somewhat similar scenes—similar, but different in that there seemed to be little assurance; different in that the cry of the heart reflected the fear that this parting was final— the fear expressed in anguished utterance: "Oh, if only we knew, if only we could be sure that it is so"—that death is conquered, that life is everlasting, that personality is forever perpetuated, that our loved ones will be there to welcome us.

These are the age-old cries and questions—the questions of Whence? and Why? and Whither?— questions concerning the open grave that have faced men from the first time death intruded into the realm of life. These questions the disciples of Jesus faced. And to the chief priests and Pharisees who requested "that the sepulchre be made sure . . ." Pilate replied, "Ye have a watch: go your way, make it as sure as ye can." [130] And so they did. But no man can secure the grave against the glorious eternal reality of everlasting life. "And when they saw him, they worshipped him: but some doubted." [131]

Yes, some doubted. Some still doubt. Some say in their loss and loneliness: "Oh, if only I knew, if only I could be sure." But you who wrestle in your souls with the question of everlasting life, take peace unto your hearts, for God has not deceived us in the assurance that the sweetest, finest things of life are everlasting, including the promised renewal of association with those we love. Scripture, logic, reason, revelation, all confirm it, with all the intimations of immortality within us, and with the added word of witnesses. He who holds creation in its course, and who brought us to birth, has not deceived us in letting us so much love life, and so much love our loved ones. Let faith overcome fear, for the question of the open grave was solved some nineteen centuries ago—and as surely as we lay away our loved ones, just so surely do they live.

The Designer ... and the Design

In some ways, time heals and softens the sharpness of many sorrows, but the sharpness of separation from our loved ones can become acute at any time, as any moment may bring its own reminders of them—especially as the years increase, especially as the long years come and go for those who live in loneliness.

Even now we know that there would really be no heaven for us without those we love, and for this reason we are inexpressibly grateful for the assurances we have of everlasting life, which makes the meaning of a day of remembrance and memorial one of looking hopefully forward, and not one of looking bitterly back.

(And even the doubter should live as if he knew that life were everlasting, because he has nothing to lose by doing so, and everything to gain. This one side-thought could well become a subject for further pursuit—but not for now.)

For now we should like to look a moment at another reassuring side of the evidence for everlasting life: In all the works of an architect or engineer or artist, we are likely to see in all of them some essential similarities. A man's distinctive mark is somehow always on his work. In some essentials each person is likely to repeat himself, and in everything he does carry over from the past some suggestion of the future.

So with the Lord God, Organizer and Designer of heaven and earth and all that in them is—surely He who made the earth would not do less than suggest something of the pattern of heaven in it. Beauty here would surely suggest something of the semblance of beauty hereafter. Love here, and the cherishing of our loved ones, would surely suggest some semblance of the pattern of cherishing our loved ones hereafter. Will companionship mean less in heaven? Will our loved ones mean less there? Will our children be less cherished?

The questions themselves suggest their own answer. And aside from all other assurances, which we accept, not doubting, and in full faith, we accept not doubting also, that God, the great Designer, will be true to His design. And since the best loved thing in life is the love and sweetness of companionship with loved ones, surely a continuance of that sweetness of association, which means so much here, is the promise and assurance that it will be so hereafter.

Doubt not, you who mourn and you who remember, that the great Designer will be true to His design.

"Not to Condemn,...but to Save..."

Of the seventh day preceding Easter, John the Beloved and others record how the multitude acknowledged the Master for what he was: the King of Israel, Messiah, and Saviour. Less than one week later, with false accusation and the mockeries of men, he was on the cross—and there was death and darkness and despair. But these were followed by dawn and light and life, by resurrection and redemption from death.

Some nineteen centuries have passed since then, and the "opposition in all things" is still sharply in evidence: Still there is the struggle of evil and good, error and truth, darkness and light, death and life. But despite all discouragements, and sometimes despair, there is the blessed reassuring certainty that the Lord God who gave us life and made us in His image will, with our willingness, lead us to further light, to fuller life, and happiness. For this cause were all the commandments given— and for this He sent His only begotten Son not to condemn, but to save the world [132]—that same beloved Son who said: "They that be whole need not a physician, but they that are sick" [133]—that same beloved Son who said: "Come unto me, all ye that labour and are heavy laden, and I will give you rest." [134] And to the sick, the suffering, the sorrowing, to the injured and offended, to the puzzled and perplexed, to those withdrawn within themselves, to the falsely dealt with and deceived, to those who have lost their loved ones, to those who live in loneliness—to all, there is help from Him who even now sits at His Father's side, and who was sent to encourage, to help, to heal, to love, to lift the lives of men, to lead the way to happiness and everlasting life.

What else would any father wish for his children? What else would we wish for our own—but happiness and everlasting life with our loved ones? And for this cause are all the counsels and commandments of God given. There are no unessential commandments, none that we can safely ignore or set aside (unless God shall withdraw it or declare it fulfilled). And blessedly, the same sure things that lead to happiness hereafter, lead also to happiness here.

We would say, in words recorded by John: "For God sent not his Son into the world to condemn the world" [132] but to save. We would say, in the words uttered at the hour of His ascension, that "this same Jesus . . . shall so come in like manner as ye have seen him go into heaven." [135] And we would say in the words of Job, but with conviction of our own: "I know that my redeemer liveth, and that he shall stand at the latter day upon the earth: And though after my skin worms destroy this body, yet in my flesh shall I see God." [136]

So Different a Day...

There is a question concerning Christmas that keeps recurring: What is it that makes it so different a day? Except for some very real and far-reaching considerations it wouldn't be so different a day—and if it weren't, we should be going through some meaningless motions.

Christmas has its own special spirit, quite apart from all other commemorative occasions. It *is* different, and there are reasons why it is and should be so. It is the day on which we have come to commemorate the birth of Jesus the Christ, the Son of God, our Saviour and our Lord, the Prince of Peace. And as concerning this, we might well consider some searching questions:

Is it just tradition? Is it just a story—or was it real? Was he born in Bethlehem of a virgin, the only Begotten of the Father in the flesh? Was there a star? Were there wise men and shepherds? Were there angels who sang? Was he what the scriptures say he was, or was he something less than the scriptures say he was?

Did he live and perform miracles and preach an immortal message? Did he heal the sick, comfort the sorrowing and confound the worldly wise? Was it so—or was it something men simply said was so?

Was he crucified and entombed, and did he rise

again the third day and appear unto his Apostles and unto others also? Did they see and touch him as was testified of Thomas?

Was he literally resurrected? Did he break the bonds of death? Did he ascend unto heaven and take his place at the right hand of the Father? Is he our Saviour and Redeemer—and will he come again? Is it all true or was it just a story—something that someone said was so?

These are questions that call for unequivocal answers, for the meaning of Christmas depends upon them. And we would witness here that the answer to each and all of them is a fervent, unequivocal, unqualified—*"Yes."* We may not altogether understand how or why, but here we would witness that He who made us in His own image, who is our loving Father, did send to earth His only begotten Son.

Were there wise men, and shepherds, and singing by the heavenly host? Was there a star? Would we be unwilling to believe that He who gave us life and who keeps creation and uncounted billions of stars in their course could place a special symbol in the sky for the birth of His beloved Son?

Even though we cannot fully understand the ultimate answers, these things we accept as we accept the fact that we are, that we live, that life is real, and that He has glorious plans and purposes for all of us that extend endlessly beyond what men now know. All this is part of the real meaning and message of Christmas, and part of what makes it so different a day.

...Always—and Forever

The longer we live the more aware we are of the shortness of this life we live, and the more aware we are of a sense of loss and of loneliness as those whom we have loved and lived among leave us one by one. And ever in the background we are aware of the questions that confront all men: Where are they? What lies beyond? Shall we know them as we knew them here?

The event to which each Easter day is dedicated is the assurance that we shall—the reality of the resurrection of Jesus the Christ, and, through him, of all others also. We read of it in scripture. We sing of it in song. We speak of it in sermon. We hold to it with full faith, but not perhaps without a gnawing wish that we could see it more certainly; not, in a sense, without wishing that we had seen with our eyes and touched with our hands as did Thomas.

But when all the evidence is before us it doesn't test our faith too far. True, we don't know how it will all be brought about. There are unanswered questions. There are difficulties that may seem insurmountable. But how many unanswered questions are there concerning other things that are all around us? How can we account for the fact that we are, that we feel, that we love, that we live? How can we account for unnumbered billions of stars that are kept in their course? for the constancy of the sun and of the seasons? for the awesome miracle of a baby's birth? for the inborn instinct of animals?

If we had never seen spring return would it not require a far-reaching of our faith to imagine that it might be so? If we had never seen trees that seemed dead one day, break forth into full flower— if we had never seen these before our eyes, these things which we have come to call commonplace— to accept them could require a far reach of our faith.

With ten times ten thousand questions that we cannot answer even about the things we can feel and touch and see, it is but a little further reach of faith to accept the reality of the resurrection and the assurance of everlasting life, and to trust Him who gave us life, to provide the way for us to see and know and live again with those we love—always and forever.

The Long Look

There seems to be little evidence that the Creator of the universe was ever in a hurry. Everywhere, on this bounteous and beautiful earth, and to the farthest reaches of the firmament, there is evidence of patient purpose and planning and working and waiting. This is a point to remember when we become too impatient with our own personal problems, or with the great unanswered questions that are in the minds of most of us.

And when our troubles trouble us too much, when our lives become too tense, it would be well to take time for a long look—out into the infinite and awesome vastness of the universe—perhaps a billion light years away, which is presently possible—across "worlds" that can't be counted—in sight of "suns" that can't be numbered—into space that can't contemplated by the mortal mind of man. "And any man who hath seen any or the least of these hath seen God moving in his majesty and power." [137]

Everywhere there is evidence of long, unhurried plan and pattern and purpose, of intelligence and continuous creation, and of the Creator—which makes one ask in all earnestness: "What is man, that thou art mindful of him?" [138] He must be important in the infinite plan and purpose or he wouldn't have the intelligence and the opportunities he has. And he is important—so much so that the Lord God made man in "his own image," [139] and has set before him limitless and everlasting possibilities.

And yet here on this pinpoint planet, the most penetrating mind among us has profound reason to feel small and humble and repentant—for with all our brilliance and accomplishment (and stupidity) we are only children on the shore of an eternal sea.

With all we know (or think we know) there is infinitely much that we must leave to time—including some of our troubles and some of our sorrows, some of our unsolved problems, and some of our unsatisfied questions. And a long look at the endless, orderly plan and purpose of the Father of us all may make some of the petty and passing things appear not so important as they have sometimes seemed. And when we find ourselves in conflict and confusion, we can well afford to wait a while for all the evidence and all the answers that now evade us.

Thank God for a glorious and interesting world, for truth, and for "infinity," and for "eternity" in which to find it—and for faith, and assurance in the limitless and everlasting future.

* * *

"Still seems it strange, that thou shouldst
    live forever?
Is it less strange, that thou shouldst live at
    all?" [140]

                    —Edward Young

Index of References to
Quoted Passages

Index of Subjects

A

[251]

[253]

Q

R

S

T